How to be a Christian Chiropractor in a Secular World

PRACTICING ABOVE
TREE TOPS

12 KEY QUESTIONS TO ASK AT EVERY
JUNCTURE OF PROFESSIONAL LIFE

CHARLES F. ROOST, D.C.

How to be a Christian Chiropractor in a Secular World

PRACTICING ABOVE
TREE TOPS

12 KEY QUESTIONS TO ASK AT EVERY
JUNCTURE OF PROFESSIONAL LIFE

CHARLES F. ROOST, D.C.

Delta Health and Wellness Center
722 N. Creyts Rd.
Lansing, MI 48917
www.DeltaHealthandWellnessCenter.com

All Scriptures are taken from the King James Bible.

Printed in the United States of America.

ISBN 978-1-257-17608-3

Printed by Calvary Publishing
A Ministry of Parker Memorial Baptist Church
1902 East Cavanaugh Road
Lansing, Michigan 48910
www.CalvaryPublishing.org

FOR BAPTISTS
BY BAPTISTS

Calvary
PUBLISHING
CP
KJV
A ministry of Parker Memorial Baptist Church
1902 East Cavanaugh Road • Lansing, Michigan 48910
Phone: 517.882.2112 • Fax: 517.882.2317

www.calvarypublishing.org

Contents

trade for a new patient?

ABOUT THE AUTHOR

D r. Roost is a Magna Cum Laude graduate of Palmer College of Chiropractic. He has been in private practice for over 30 years, and is actively involved in the leadership of 5 different Non-Profit Organization boards, including the Christian Chiropractors Association, Rescue Southern Sudan Village People, The Foundation for the Advancement of Healthy Aging, and Global Outreach Development.

He founded the Michigan Christian Chiropractors Association and heads up a free clinic in conjunction with the Lansing City Rescue Mission. He has participated in, and helped direct 9 mission trips in 6 different countries.

His practice, Delta Chiropractic Center, has served thousands of patients, and has averaged well over 225 patient visits per week over those 30 plus years. In those three decades he has adjusted over 350,000 people, delivering over a million specific spinal adjustments. He and his staff are the team Chiropractors for the Capital City Stealth, Crown Gym and other sports teams. He enjoys speaking and teaching on subjects such as stress management, goal setting, and other health related topics.

He has mentored 6 newly graduated Chiropractors in his practice over those years. His office employs 6 staff members, and this staff of highly motivated assistants agree that their office plants effective seeds for spiritual growth in the hearts of their patients.

His other books include two fiction works, and a wellness guide book titled, *Reservoir of Better Health.*

Dedication:

How do you make a list of people to thank, when the people who have brought you to this place stretch over a lifetime? I offer a huge thank you to those who have led and supported and taught Judi and me what we have needed to know when we needed to know it. My gratitude starts and ends with the Holy Spirit, who teaches us all things. And in between that start and finish – thanks to my wife, who has led at times, and learned along with me the rest of the time. I am so blessed with her at my side. Then, thanks to others who have dug into the Word, and then faithfully passed on truth – Brother Keith Moore, who unknowingly fed us all the way from Missouri, Duane Feldpausch, who chewed it up and organized it some more, Pastor Michael DeBose, who faithfully prepares and shares spiritual meals with us each Sunday, and Doctor Larry Green, who shared some of his 50 plus years of deep wisdom and experience, and graciously rejoiced in the possibilities of this book.

Finally, a quiet thank you to Tom Fitzsimmons, who opened the door of this information through his battle and struggle – so bravely fought. We miss you here.

Introduction:

Practicing above the treetops

Question Number One: What will motivate my life – self, or Christ?

Any Chiropractic practice can be described as either, "This is the life!" or "Living the life". When person makes the choice to become a Chiropractor, it is a watershed decision. But it's only the beginning, because there are many, many more decisions to make. Where to go to school. Whether to specialize. Where to practice. What style of practice in which to invest your professional life. What equipment to use and how to finance it. What hours to keep. Who to hire as help. But none of those decisions are as important in shaping the value of the rest of your professional life as is framing your purpose.

Take the time to write out your purpose – your mission statement. This project will require a time of introspection, a time of asking yourself some soul-searching, heart-baring questions. So with a fresh sheet of clean, white paper, ask yourself these questions.

1. What do I want to accomplish with my life?
2. What kind of people do I work best with?
3. When I get to the end of my life, what do I hope people will say about me?

(In The Seven Habits of Highly Effective People by Stephen Covey, there is an exercise described that can help with this mental picture. Envision yourself as an observer at your own funeral. Imagine four people speaking about you at the service, one family member, one colleague, one friend, and one knows you from your community involvement o, your church. What would each one say about you? And how should you live your life to bring about such a description of your life?)

1. What are your greatest gifts, talents, skills?
2. What are the weakest areas in your life?
3. How can you best serve God and mankind?
4. What did God equip you with, and what did He equip you to do?
5. How can I organize my life in such a way as to make sure the important things get done consistently?
6. How can I make sure there is a wise balance between relationships and work, between contributing to my world, and leaving behind a heritage and example for those who follow after?

Asking, pondering and answering the questions that define your purpose, mission, vision, and attitude will direct and shape the style and satisfaction, as well as the enduring fruit of what you do with your life as a Chiropractor. Take the time to formulate a mission statement, and then think about each of the roles you play in life – spouse, parent, doctor, church member, friend, citizen. These examples of roles are just thought starters. Think about your own life, and come up with titles for the major roles of your own life.

I have found the process of writing my mission

statement to be an intimidating challenge. How do you put into a sentence, the meaning of your life? Yet the process has brought clarity to my life when I've been at points in my life where I wondered what to do, what to say 'no' to, what was the value of my life, and how I could make the best use of my time here.

In the process I sometimes thought it would be helpful to see other's mission statement. It would put some parameters on what was expected of such an assignment. But, in hind sight, I have come to the conclusion that seeing other mission statement causes two negative results – it may superimpose the values of others onto the image of what God is molding you into, causing your words to reflect either too broadly or too narrowly, or in a different direction altogether, what God wants to do in your life.

So I recommend that you not look for examples to spur your thinking. Start fresh. For more help in the process, I found The Seven Habits of Highly Effective People to be helpful. Then, once you have some words down on paper, if you would like to see the current form of my mission statement, drop me a line, and I'll be happy to e-mail you a copy.

How does your mission statement mold your interactions, relationships, and even your to-do list in each of those roles? This project of formulating your life's mission statement will determine if your life will be significant or merely 'another life' come and gone with nothing to show for it. Once this is done, you may then find more value in contemplating the questions we consider in this book. It will also help you sort through the impact your professional title will have on your life.

In almost any culture on the planet, the title "Doctor" carries with it an automatic credibility, respect and honor that encourage most people to treat the health care professional as a sort of a minor deity. The title, and the ensuing semi-worship that is lavished upon the physician, become a strong temptation for the man or woman with the title to expect honor as their due. All too often the Chiropractor comes to expect that honor as though they were born higher and better than all others. Along with this sense of entitlement usually comes a higher financial standard of living. Thus, the decision must be consciously made to either live to maximize that 'life on a pedestal', focusing on building the kingdom of 'self', or to answer the biblical call to live a life of wise stewardship of time, talent and treasure, investing these resources into the kingdom of God.

Will you, doctor, give a self-satisfied sigh and settle into a mindset of "This is the life", or will you humbly choose to sacrifice your pride, and live the life that Christ purchased for you? Thus we come to the first key question each of us must ask ourselves: "What will motivate my life – self, or Christ?" This is a fundamental question – a foundational issue that must be addressed and answered if you hope to live a life that matters. Unanswered, this question will hang there like a broken rudder on a ship. Without knowing your own answer to this, you will flounder through your career with no direction. You will reach the end of your career in a few short decades, look back over your life, and wonder, "What just happened?" At that point, the questions have been answered for you, and you will not like the way they flow across the screen as the credits roll.

I see an interesting analogy in the way that question is answered – a mirror image between the blessed, advantage-filled life of a Chiropractic physician and the way the United States was blessed in her history. A quick look at her history will show how the United States of America was born and grew into great blessing and then squandered it on selfishness and pride. The freedoms, natural resources, human giftedness, and place in history that this country was given were used initially to welcome needy people from all around the world, and to pour those blessings back into a world that was so hungry for them. All too soon, however, the blessings brought a mindset of deservedness, an attitude of avarice, and a protective mental separation between 'we the haves' and 'they the have-nots'. No longer sharing the blessings, the U.S., through selfish squandering of her blessings, has entered a twilight of dwindling freedoms and blessings that will be difficult to reverse.

Chiropractor, guard your heart! For the same attitudes creep into the heart of many who gain the education and credibility that make up a physician's career. Decide early in your professional life to invest your gifts into the lives of others. Or, if you are decades into your career, decide anew – it is not too late to begin trading your skills and time for eternal return rather than for money, power, or the respect of men. It is not too late to see your practice become the fount of blessings, healing, and spiritual insight that God meant it to be.

There are other questions that will shape your life as a Chiropractor. Not just the practical questions mentioned in the first paragraph of this introduction, but deeper, character-shaping questions. In this book we will walk through eleven more of those questions, and the implications of their answers. But stop first – take a moment now, and ask yourself, "What will drive the rest of my career as a Chiropractor – self, or Christ?"

Then, as you answer the questions in each chapter take a moment to ask for wisdom. God tells us that it is ours for the asking. Solomon said that wisdom is calling out to us, and that when we find her, she appears with long life in one hand, and riches and honor in the other. (Proverbs 3:16) Surely she is worth seeking. So ask for it. Get it. And prosper.

Being led by the Holy Spirit in a practical, specific way is the answer to all of life's questions, so don't read the questions and then rely only on your mind to answer. Ask and listen for His wisdom and for the best answer for each question.

Section 1 - Running A Christian Practice

Chapter 1

Practicing Above the Tree Tops

Question Number Two: What sets you, as a Christian Chiropractor, apart from any other ethical Chiropractor?

Every Chiropractor should be living and practicing in a way that is professional and exemplifies a lifestyle that encourages people to live well. There is a standard for ethics imposed upon all professionals that is above the norm for non-professional people. The influence that a professional has in their community requires that they live up to a level of ethics – an example that people find – well – exemplary. This is true for every Chiropractor – Christian or not. It is a standard set by statute for all professionals in each state. Morally, legally, and ethically, every Chiropractor is expected to live a life that stays above a certain measure, simply because they are a professional and are, as such, given trust by the public.

Think of this level of professional ethics as the tree top level, the canopy of a vast forest viewed from 10,000 feet, at which all professionals should function and live. And if that is the tree top level against which we compare ourselves – if that is the bar against which we are measured – then at what level should a Christ follower function? What makes a Christian's life stand out in such a way that makes people see, and desire, a difference? What about a Christian Chiropractor is different – better than the average? Sure, a professional should provide a good example with his life, but I submit that this should be even more evident of every man or woman who purports to follow Christ. A Chiropractor who knows Christ should live and practice in such a way that they:

- Shed light in a dark world
- Stimulate hunger for a better life in those who watch
- Live with unimpeachable integrity
- Trade their time for things of eternal value

So how do we do that? I suggest that this is part of the definition of living the "abundant life" that Christ promised us as His followers. And if this is true, how do we live abundantly? How do we express a life full of Christ and still run a successful business? How do we strive to live above the level of professionalism at which every non-Christian Chiropractor should be living?

There is a way. In fact, there are likely many ways. We are all gifted with different personalities, skills, talents, experiences and bents that will drive how we practice. In this vein there are several facets of our practices of which we should be aware, and in which we should live Christ-like within our practices.

Over the next four chapters we will discuss how we

can "practice above the treetops" – living in such a way that patients, as well as other Chiropractors, can look on and wonder what we've got that allows us to live in such an appealing way. Ways to let our God-reflected light shine. Ways to be a 'city on a hill', beckoning wanderers from wasted lives into lives that satisfy. Ways to be tasteful salt in a tasteless world.

In section one of our look at running a Christian Chiropractic practice, we will explore four areas in which you can go from just being a good Chiropractor, to being a good Christian Chiropractor, including:

1) Atmosphere
2) Integrity
3) Staffing issues
4) Sharing the gospel

These four aspects of practice can lead to practicing above the level of the tree tops. They are not all-inclusive, but are a strong start to letting God use you in ways that stand out. You want your life to count? Practice with an intentional awareness of these areas, an awareness of issues that can set you apart. Don't just let life go by! Live it with purpose, on purpose, and with a determination to live above.

Prayerfully consider the issues for yourself. You will find that the Holy Spirit will point you toward areas in which you can live above the level of the tree tops. He will show you how you can uniquely be a light in your office. Then, as He entrusts lives to your care in the form of patients and friends and colleagues, your interaction with them will be seed for changed lives.

Chapter 2

Practicing Above the Tree Tops – 1

Running A Christian Practice With Atmosphere

Question Number Three: What does your office say, shout, or whisper to the people who enter?

While we DCs, as professionals in our respective communities, should function responsibly and with integrity, it is also true that we Chiropractors who are Christians should live above that level of professionalism. We are referring to that lifestyle as 'practicing above the tree tops' – living a lifestyle that is ethically above the level of a merely moral Chiropractor – a lifestyle that stands out as a Christ follower. As a part of being a light in the world, and in an effort to be a witness to our patients as well as to our peers, we must 'be mature and fully developed' in our faith walk. Granted, this is a tall order, but the Word commands it so, by His grace, we can do it.

Practically speaking, what does that look like in the office? As we answer our third key question, we will discuss the first aspect of practicing above the tree tops. You might think that the starting point of that lifestyle might be 'witnessing' to those around us. But I suggest that, before we ever say a word about Christ, we need to earn the right to do that by living a life that demonstrates that we offer something different – something better than just another good Chiropractor! One of the ways we do that is by the first impression we make on the people who enter our office for their initial visit. There is no need to spend tons of cash on the image factor of our practice, but we cannot ignore it either.

Each of us has fallen into the trap of allowing a first impression to set the stage for how we view a person. The young man who walks around with dreadlocks and tattoos may be a computer genius who can set you up with a killer web site. But it is much harder for him to get the chance to prove it when he presents himself in that way. The same is true when someone first encounters you and your office.

So the starting point in running a Christian practice has to do with the atmosphere of your practice. When a patient walks into your practice, what do they experience? Once a month, doctor, take 5 minutes, walk into the front door of your office, and experience the reception area as a patient would. Walk in, look around, take a seat. What do you see? Smell? Hear? Are you greeted with a smile and 'hello' immediately? Are the corners cobweb free? Is there dust around the feet of the chairs? Is the music uplifting? Is the bathroom clean and fresh smelling? Are the magazines congruent with what you live and believe?

Walls must also hold information that is congruent with what you teach. Pictures and posters should trigger thoughts that point conversation toward improving health. None of this shouts "I am a Christian, and you should be too!" But it is an important component of setting the stage for such a message.

Of course all of this must be built upon the solid foundation of your mission in life. And that mission – the purpose for which you are in business and in practice – must be tied, theoretically and practically, to what Jesus said was most important – loving God and loving people. Take a moment right now to think about your answers to the mission statement questions in the introduction.

Having answered these questions, shift now to a broader question. Can you write out in one sentence the reason why you are in practice? Why do you get up and out of bed in the morning? What do you feel passionate about? Does your purpose take you above the level of merely earning a living to impacting your world for eternity? This defines a live of significance.

Albert Schweitzer said once, "I don't know what your destiny will be, but one thing I do know: the only ones among you who will be really happy are those who have sought and found how to serve." Obviously a man of insight. In light of this, keep in mind the importance of serving people in significant ways as you write out your mission in life.

If you can't write your mission statement out in the form of a short paragraph of purpose, then you must spend some time thinking through what you do and why you do it. Find an hour of quiet time, grab a pen and a pad of paper, sit down and write it out. Tweak it, rewrite it, and re-rewrite it again until it resonates within your heart. This solidifies and focuses the attitude and direction of your heart and your actions.

And what of the attitude behind the front desk? The staff must also believe that what they are doing is positive and important. They must know and understand your purpose statement, and agree with it. They must know that what your office offers people is good and right. They must know in their hearts that what the patient is experiencing is real and important. During office hours, they must focus on the patient more than on their own life drama.

And finally, your efforts must strive toward excellence. You must never rely on what you knew and did yesterday to set your standard of care. Whether you graduated last month, or 30 years ago, you must continue to hone your skills. A huge reservoir of knowledge is not the end all of what you can offer people, but current, cutting-edge skills will bring more healing skills to your tool kit, allowing you to do a better job of assisting people in their search for better health.

In practice, your exam protocols must be excellent, current, and relevant to what the patient is experiencing, and relevant to what you are offering them in the effort to improve their symptoms and activities of daily living. Your exam should be designed to uncover the causes of their problems, and to measure improvements over the course of their treatment. Changes in office protocols, in the areas of examination and treatment, are not generally fun for the doctor or the staff, but if you are still using the same protocols you did even 10 years ago, you are missing new, and potentially better techniques and technology. You must invest in your skills and knowledge to stay excellent at what you do.

Practicing above the tree tops – establishing an atmosphere in the office that shines as a light to those who enter – that is a crucial part of running a practice that is not merely good Chiropractic, but Christ-like Chiropractic. What does your office say, shout, or whisper to the people who enter? Ask yourself this question, but answer it from a fresh perspective. How would a new patient answer it? How do your spouse and staff answer it?

The atmosphere of your office should typically only whisper the message that you are different. But it should still consistently and quietly communicate the message – "We are different here". "We practice in a different way, for reasons that will be clear soon." The message should start a thought process in those who encounter it. They should start to wonder about you, doctor. They should start to sense that there is something different, something good, something intriguing and appetizing here.

Aim to practice in an atmosphere of excellent, Christ-like professionalism to set the stage for life-impacting, hunger-inducing lifestyle.

Chapter 3

Practicing Above the Tree Tops Two

Running A Christian Practice With Integrity

Question Number Four: Is it ever ethical to cheat, cut corners, or lie?

We've discussed the idea of practicing above the tree tops – above the level of ethics and kindness that is expected of all professionals. As representatives of both Chiropractic and Christ, we must live and practice above the ethical level at which everyone else lives if we expect to impact our world for Christ.

As we discussed in the last chapter, one way we do that is to set an atmosphere of excellence in our surroundings. The physical setting, as well as the attitude with which we approach situations and people must be beyond good, they must be great – focused, purposeful, intentional, and eternity-minded.

The next aspect of living at that 'altitude' is the matter of integrity. Absolute integrity – doing the right thing even if it hurts, even if it costs, even if no one else is watching – is the bedrock of ethics. And if we do what is right even when no one else is there to see it, we will do right when there are others around watching as well.

There are many areas in which our integrity will be tested. Responding to those tests with absolute integrity will show itself in many ways also. They can be summed up in a couple simple rules, excerpted from the writings of Richard Mayberry:

1) Do all you promise to do
2) Do not infringe on other people's property

If you think about it, almost all rules of ethics and morality, and almost all laws, can be integrated under, or extrapolated from these two laws. Most civil laws descend from these rules: tort or contractual law comes from the first rule. Basically, your word should be good even without a written contract and a court full of lawyers to enforce it. Criminal law comes from the second (don't steal, kill, trespass, etc.) This is an extrapolation of the Golden Rule, and derives from a mindset of valuing other's rights as you would want your own rights valued.

I think though, that we should get a bit more specific in how they impact your office. So let's discuss a couple practical office protocols that hinge on integrity.

One area where integrity is tested in the office setting is the area of office finances. I am amazed, but no longer surprised, at what money does to people's integrity. People who you would think were above temptation will bend rules and sell their integrity for a few extra dollars. This piece of your integrity will be put to the test in two areas in your office – your billing practices with insurance companies and with patients.

In your relationships with insurance companies you

are bound by the agreements you signed in order to participate with them. These are contractual agreements that spell out how you must bill for services. Did you agree to bill only for covered services? Then do what you said you would do. Did you agree to write off everything above what they say they will cover – to your loss? Then write it off. (Argh! I hate this one. 'I performed an excellent service with high professional standards and great outcome, and then I can't collect reasonable fees for it?') The other option is to not participate – though, obviously that brings in new challenges of attracting patients who have that insurance coverage and expect you to participate. How many times have you heard the question, "Do you take my insurance?"

How about writing off copays? Do you embrace the old 'NOOPE' idea? Or do you collect patient copays? It is the law – in most states, and at the federal level. This concept ties in with Medicare and Medicaid law concerning "Inducements". You cannot give patients anything valued over $10 per visit, nor over $50 per year in an effort to encourage them to come in for care. Writing off a patient's copay falls under this law, as well as under the contractual agreement with the insurance company you signed with. We cannot legally write off patient copays under government insured plans as an across the board policy. Many experts believe that this is also true for all other insurance agreements, though some feel it does not cross over to private insurance companies. Check with your own legal counsel for clarity in your geographic area.

You can, in cases of financial hardship, agree with a patient, on a one-on-one basis, to waive their copay. But remember, to do it across the board is illegal. Don't do it, or you run the risk of fines, post payment audits and reimbursements, loss of participation rights with those insurance companies, potentially the loss of your license, and of course the loss of your integrity. Your services are worth what you charge for them – all of it. Your integrity is worth far more than a copay, so collect the full fee allowed under your contractual agreements with the insurance companies and the patient.

Finally, under the topic of integrity, let us purpose to tell our patients the truth. Let us tell them the truth about our charges, about their condition, about their options for care, about the pros and cons concerning those options, and about our intentions. I often enjoy telling them the negative side effects of medicine and surgery (perhaps I enjoy this too much?), but it's just as important to reveal to them any potential negatives about our own treatments, too.

Be totally transparent with your patients right from their initial phone contact and consultation. Let them know the benefits of your care, what that care will entail, how much it will cost, what other options there are, the benefits to those options (and of course the risks to those options). In most cases the benefits to taking advantage of your care will far outweigh the other options, and you will find your practice filling up with great patients who trust you, take your advice, and respond well. With that as the foundation to your doctor/patient relationship, you will see them willing to pay for their care, and to refer others just like them.

Another facet of this topic is your willingness to tell a patient if you don't think they are a good candidate for your care or your office. They may not have a condition you are qualified to treat effectively. They may not be willing to pay for your care. They may just not fit with the atmosphere of your office. Any of these factors may disqualify a patient from beginning care in your office, but it is better to not start a doctor/patient relationship, than it is to begin one and then have to dissolve it. I know there are times when I've accepted a patient against my inner feelings that I shouldn't have, and then regretted it later when they got upset because of a personality difference, or a miscommunication. Writing a letter to terminate care, and asking them to seek care elsewhere is not pleasant, nor is it an experience that promotes good word of mouth advertising or referrals.

For any of these reasons, you, the doctor, must enter the consultation with a willingness to tell them that they might find more effective care elsewhere. Be prepared with a list of professionals you trust to whom you can refer them. The actual number of consultations that end this way is very small, but being ready to have the discussion places you in a much healthier position as the physician.

Integrity is a key component to practicing above the tree tops. When finances, insurance hassles, or panic over an empty appointment book drive your clinical decisions or our billing practices, you are in danger of selling out your integrity. Watch for it, recognize it, and correct it if it's there.

Is it ever ethical to cheat, cut corners or lie? This may be a good time to ask the all too often flippantly used question, "What would Jesus do?" It is easy to say the 'right' answer. But to recognize the problems in our own hearts and practices can be challenging because they usually show up gradually and subtly. And our flesh, left unchecked, can rationalize a lot of poor decision making. Take the time to search out an honest answer. "Search me, oh God, and know my heart, try me and show me my inner ways."

So, how do we build a healthy practice, helping as many people as we can with the time given to us in a lifetime while still maintaining integrity? Simple! Do all you promise to do, and do not infringe on others people's property. Or, as some wise person recommended – aim to under promise and over deliver, and your patients will always leave happy.

Chapter 4

Practicing Above the Tree Tops – 3

Running A Christian Practice With Staffing

Question Number Five: Why did you hire the staff you hired? / What do you expect out of your staff?

So, how are we doing? Check yourself – how far above the level of just a "mere mortal" (1 Corinthians 3:3) are you living? If the top of your 'tree' is the same height as every other Chiropractor in your city, what is it that sets you apart from them? Where is the salt and light that makes you appealing to those watching your life? There are many nice, honest, happy Chiropractors. What makes your life more attractive than theirs? In what ways are you practicing above the level of the tree tops around you? Not necessarily in total collections or patient volume, but in atmosphere, attitude, integrity, excellence, and in personnel.

In exploring this idea, we've already discussed the atmosphere of your office, and the integrity of your business and professional actions, but we still haven't even mentioned overt witnessing in the office. Before we get to what many would think is the very first segment of a Christian's life that would set them apart from any other professional's office, let's finish setting the stage for that key component of living above the tree tops.

It is appropriate to spend a few moments discussing hiring and staff. If your office is to stand out as a Christian witness in a secular world, you must be very careful about who represents you in the front office. The staff is, after all, the first and last contact each patient has with your office. It is their friendly greetings, clear instructions, and skillful handling of accounts that will leave an impression in patients' minds. I know Chiropractors want to believe that patients all come to your office because of your skill and wisdom and high quality lumbar roll, but the truth is, many patients return to your office just because of our kind-hearted staff. And unfortunately, many of them refuse to return because of a bad interaction with a staff member.

In hiring staff, you must be completely intentional. There are only two reasons to decide who to hire: either the prospective staff member is a Christian who will represent you in as Christ-like a manner as you do yourself, or they are unsaved, and are, therefore, another person to whom you are representing Christ – hopefully leading to salvation. (There is actually a third reason to hire a person – it's called nepotism, but I can't say that or my sister-in-law, who happens to be my office manager, will quit.)

So, not every staff person must be a Christian. Skills, personality, reliability and enthusiasm are important in any hire, but beyond that, if you are to have a kingdom mindset in running your practice, you must also think of your staff with their eternal destination in mind, too.

There is no question that every person employed by your office does represent you to patients and to anyone else with whom your office comes into contact. Therefore, they must live at the same high level of integrity and lifestyle that you want the office to express – whether they are already saved or not.

In addition, if you want your office to impact patients for Christ, it is imperative that each team member be on the same page with the mission and purpose you have developed. At the very least, each staff member must present a positive, encouraging personality, bringing joy and edification with every patient encounter. Right from the first interview, you should make clear what you value in a staff member. In our staff policies we list three: Timeliness, Integrity, and Self Direction.

Other things to encourage in your staff team? Greeting each patient with an enthusiastic smile and cheerful word of welcome when they enter your office is important. Whatever your staff is doing at the front desk, they should stop that task, and greet each person walking through the door immediately. Answering the phone with a smile behind the voice may never be seen, but it will be heard. It may feel funny at first, but smiling on the phone changes tone every time, regardless of how you are feeling. You really can 'hear' a smile on the other end of the line.

Filling quiet moments with a list of minor chores like filing, cleaning, double checking the postings from earlier in the day, making sure all supplies, print cartridges, paper products, and x-ray supplies are ordered in a timely fashion, will keep any office running smoothly. And your staff should recognize that they can step up and do these functions regularly without having to be told each step of the way.

These ideas and skills and job lists can be honed and reviewed in staff meetings. For this, and many other reasons, staff meetings are an important tool in forging a cohesive unit, and common vision among your team. Use regular staff meetings for fine tuning team interaction, learning how to handle common situations, and for reminding each team member of your goals, vision, and mission. Staff meetings can be a fun, uplifting time for all, and therefore should not be the place for correction, discipline or "smack downs" for mistakes. Save correction for private, one-on-one moments. Remember, praise in public, and correct in private.

If you are convinced your staff is tracking with your desire to impact patients spiritually, you may feel comfortable in giving them the latitude to take advantage of appropriate moments in patient flow to encourage them, or to pray with them. We keep a small box in the adjusting rooms into which patients can deposit written prayer requests or suggestions. Of course, staff should be careful to keep such interactions private, and to keep the doctor apprised of what is going on in this area of patient relationships.

Ask yourself, "Why did you hire the staff you hired?

/ What do you expect out of your staff?" Staff is a key component in any successful office. In operating at a level above the tree tops, they serve a unique purpose. Choose prayerfully and carefully, and train regularly and thoroughly.

Chapter 5

Practicing Above the Tree Tops – 5

Running A Christian Practice and Sharing the Gospel

Question Number Six: At what point do we shift from 'being light', to sharing the word?

In Christian offices, we must attempt to set a standard – a zesty, tasty lifestyle that will give patients a "hunger for what you got". We've discussed the importance of several factors in creating an atmosphere in which the gospel can be shared with credibility:

1) The atmosphere of the office
2) The absolute integrity of our actions and words
3) The wonderful staff that God has brought together, who reflect the same standards and vision that keep you going each day

These are crucial factors that we can look at as parts of living life at a level above the norm. We've termed this "Practicing Above the Tree Tops", or functioning at a level of professionalism and excellence that is beyond what is expected of every professional in our great career of Chiropractic. These factors bear witness to your character, and are important in themselves. Beyond merely living with an impeccable character, however, they also earn you the right to take the next step.

Sharing Christ with people can be like throwing cold water on a shivering person, or may be welcomed as a meal to a starving man. The difference between rejection of your 'accusation', and reception of your 'words of hope', may rest on whether we've prepared ourselves with the ability to handle the Word accurately, it may be a matter of waiting for the timing of the Holy Spirit, or it may very well be in how we've set the stage. Have you built a stable platform from which you can share with credibility, or not? A platform of atmosphere, integrity, and excellent staff support?

If you have managed to be 'in the zone' with these three prerequisites, the next stage is simple and will come naturally. No forcing, no faking, just sharing what is in your hearts.

It starts with your first interaction with each new patient, and may continue, as the Spirit leads, through the entire start-to-end relationship with the patient. But if your heart is right in the matter of loving people by valuing their eternal destiny, you will find comfortable ways to have portions of the gospel available in each conversation. At the same time, the gospel should never be forced into a conversation, rather, the gospel, being such an integral part of your heart, will unfold in each conversation naturally.

In my office, our new patient paperwork 'front loads' the importance of the spiritual factor of life by asking the patient to rate their spiritual interest. This shows up as a question that is located in the same series of questions that rate their energy level, flexibility and pain levels. It is simply one of 10 questions that asks the patient to circle their own evaluation of how interested in spiritual matters they are.

Next, our New Patient consultation includes a matter-of-fact introduction to spiritual matters by talking about the importance of spiritual health to being truly physically healthy. We briefly mention six areas of health that will impact their wellness –

1) Nutrition,
2) Rest,
3) Exercise,
4) stress management,
5) Spiritual health, and
6) The function of the spine.

The consultation is an important moment in the relationship between the patient and the doctor, because we have the opportunity to develop a sense of how comfortable each patient is with discussing spiritual matters, which in turn helps us know how circumspect we must be as we continue the discussion of spiritual matters further along in our interactions. Sensitivity to this can prevent us from pushing too hard, or "scaring off the patient" by dwelling too long on spiritual matters when they are not yet ready for them.

The next opportunity occurs during the report of findings. In our office, this takes place on each patient's second visit. At that time, each patient is given a written report of our findings and recommendations in which there is a short paragraph on spiritual health. We also insert into their take-home packet a paper that discusses the plan of salvation. This paper actually has three different editions – each a short essay on spiritual health. One is for a person who indicates "NO" or "LITTLE" interest in spiritual matters on their intake paperwork. The second is for the person who indicates a "MODERATE" level of interest. And the third is written with the person with "GREAT" interest in mind. These essays are included in Appendix A if you'd like to see how we address these issues.

The opportunity to sow spiritual seed with patients does not end at the report of findings, however. We require each new patient to attend a workshop at which we teach spinal exercises, nutritional guidelines, stress management concepts and so on. We address each of the six building blocks for good health mentioned above: Nutrition, Rest, Exercise, Stress Management, Spinal Health, and Spiritual Health. At these workshops we cover practical ways to improve patient health in each of these areas. The spiritual component includes a very brief overview of the Bible, what Jesus did at the cross, and the importance of faith. We keep this short, but practical, and encourage each patient to make a small, achievable goal for each of the six areas we covered. The spiritual component is non-confrontational, yet tells exactly what I believe is important in the Word – that people take advantage of what Jesus did at the cross.

All through their care, we as a team are aware of our patients' need for prayer. We pray for them each morning as a team, and also pray with them when the Spirit leads us to offer it. In 30 years of practice, I've had only one patient refuse prayer when I offered it. It felt awkward for a moment when he said 'No' to my offer. But I simply went on with the rest of the office visit, and scheduled him for his next appointment.

I've also had 2 (that I know of) patients so offended by our Christian content that they dropped out of care for that reason. One of them sent a polite card explaining his concerns, and I wrote back to let him know that he could have copies of his records, and that he was always welcome back if he wanted our help in the future. He did not return to our office, but I suppose, if a patient is going to be offended in our office, I'd rather have it be over the gospel than over any other issue. Yet, even those who left our practice were gently exposed to the gospel at least twice.

Just as impactful, let me recommend short term mission trips as a last form of witness in the office. These trips are a great conversation starter for patients who wonder why you would give up a couple weeks of your life to go to a poor area and donate your expertise and finances. Patients love knowing that their doctor is selfless enough to go, and often enjoy contributing finances or gifts to make your trip more effective. (For more information on sort-term Chiropractic missions opportunities, contact the Christian Chiropractors Association at www.christianchiropractors.org or (800) 999-1979.) Also, since technology has made it so easy, we share either video or a power point slide show of the trip in our reception area after my return.

In addition to all of this, I believe that donating time

to a mission trip is a form of sowing seeds that will bear a harvest in our practices in several ways – increasing awareness in our patients, drawing more new patients into the practice, and more.

So the question stands: At what point in a life of show and tell does the 'show' become 'tell'? Do we ever speak up? Are we bold enough to obey when the Spirit says, "This person is ready. Tell them about me." I remember a conversation with my father in which he told me that one of his regrets in his Christian life is that he fell for the idea of living a good life and waiting for someone to ask him, "What makes your life different?" They never have.

Now, I've heard anecdotal stories of people who have had such a question asked of them in response to a "good Christian lifestyle", but those stories are as common as people showing up symptom free in your office asking for lifetime care and pre-paying for it in cash. I suspect that if that is the sole way for evangelism to occur, we'll have an awfully small crowd in heaven.

Do we verbalize the hope we have in Christ? If not, the answer to the question, "Why not?" is important. Because, if we are not sharing because we are embarrassed or ashamed of the gospel, the Word says He will be ashamed of us. If we neglect to speak up because we are afraid it may cost us a paying patient, then we are guilty of putting our desire for money over concern for the eternal condition of another human. If that is the case, perhaps we ought to be ashamed of ourselves.

In any case, we are blessed with a profession that is a natural platform for caring for people, not just physically, but also spiritually. Let us not squander that platform, nor those opportunities, missing them for merely a good career, a large practice, for being 'liked' by people, or for popularity.

There we have it – four aspects of practice in which we set ourselves above the level of all the good, nice, ethical Chiropractors in our cities. Six questions that will help shape our future when we take the time to ponder and answer them. Salt and light. Practicing above the tree tops so that others can see, and hungrily desire, what it is that makes our lives different.

Section 2

Ethical Practice Building

Living above the level of the tree tops does not necessarily require building a huge, financially rich practice. Just the same, we must learn to run a healthy business at the same time we are ministering to people's needs in our practices, or we will soon find ourselves out of practice completely. So I think we can all agree that living above the tree tops does include managing a successful practice.

In the course of my experience with the Christian Chiropractors' Association I had the opportunity to respond to the questions of a new graduate from a Chiropractic school. The questions revolved around the process of and decisions made in going into practice for the first time. As we begin this next section of running a Christian practice, the e-mails written back and forth may be a useful introduction to the topic of growing a healthy Christian Chiropractic practice.

(Details of the e-mails have been changed a bit to blur identities, and to clarify what was shared.)

Chapter 6

Five E-mails to a New Doc

ONE – 1

Dear Doctor Storyl,

Congratulations on your new degree, and on the new chapter in your life. How exciting! It's great to hear of another Christian Chiropractor getting into the quest for better health for people. And the cool part about what we do is that we get to help people, not just physically, through a great profession, but we also have a perfect platform from which to help people spiritually as well. What a blessing to be in this profession.

You are in a rare position - just setting up your practice. Starting fresh, you get to do it your way. Understandably, you want to do it right - with the knowledge and skill sets needed to build a business, and one that is both successful and honoring to God. As you can imagine, there is a lot that goes into that. Building such a practice includes smooth systems that cover potential issues before they happen, clear education for your patients that teaches them how to heal, comply with your recommendations and refer others, complete paperwork that is organized and covers the legal and insurance requirements, equipment, employees, taxes and accounting, insurance...

A huge part of the success of your healthy, growing business is patient education. And, done right, patient education can be a tool that plants spiritual seed in a non-threatening way at the same time it teaches them about physical health. I use a six-part approach with my patients right from the initial paperwork, through the consultation, report of findings, 'new patient workshop', ongoing care and progress report. The six areas of health that we try to teach patients about are:

- Nutrition
- Rest
- Exercise
- Stress Management
- Spiritual Health
- Nerve Health

As far as the systems that we use to evaluate and teach on these areas, they are broad - and at least difficult, if not impossible to teach in this letter-by-letter format. I have no problems with sharing them with you, but they are pretty involved. So what do we do with that? A few options.

1) I can send you pieces of it by mail, and hope I can convey how they are used.
2) You are welcome to visit our office to go through them as we use them here.
3) You can develop your own – a great option, because then you will know and 'own' the material. It is much easier to teach material that you personally own.

Whew! That's a lot to put into an e-mail, but there you go. Let me know if we can assist in any way.

Blessings on you as you follow the Lord in impacting your part of the world for Christ!
Dr. Chuck Roost

TWO - 2

Dr. Storyl,
I forget, are you starting a new practice from scratch, working with someone else, or purchasing a practice?

In any case, the four keys to building a practice are:

New Patients
Patient Retention
Other revenue (nutrition, supports, etc.)
Overhead and Financial planning

I think your initial questions dealt mostly with item number two, so I'll direct my thoughts in that direction until you tell me otherwise.

Patient retention starts with your first contact with the potential patient. You want to frame your marketing and your interactions with potential patients in such a way that they:

- Reflect the things that make you and your practice unique

- Set the stage for education and for expectations - both yours and theirs

The key to patient retention is educating them on the benefits of the care you are recommending, and then making clear recommendations. Starting with your paperwork, and continuing with your consultation, report of findings, every visit, and your new patient group class/workshop, you must teach, test their understanding, and re-teach health building blocks to each patient. Building into them an understanding of the importance of your regular care, and the importance of working in all six areas of real health, takes clear and repeated teaching. (Do you remember what the six areas of health are? Nutrition, Rest, Exercise, Stress Management, Spiritual Health, Nerve Integrity.)

You will gradually find your own ways of teaching these, and you will develop a deeper sensitivity for when people are ready for more of each one.

In the mean time - any questions? What would you like next? Forms, Scripts, Power Point for workshops?

Let me know, and I'll try to supply what has worked for me.

Blessings,

Dr. Chuck Roost

THREE – 3

Dr. Storyl,

When I went into practice I bought a small practice,

which gave me a good jump start. I got a good deal on it, so it wasn't a huge financial hurdle. That can be a good way to go. But so can starting fresh or going with an independent contractor relationship. Each of these options has its benefits and risks. I don't recommend a pure associateship because you will spend an extended period of time being overworked and underpaid, usually building nothing of lasting value that you can take with you. You can probably learn just as much volunteering at a busy office for a few weeks if you go there with open eyes and a willingness to learn.

Keep me posted as you sort through your options, and if you have questions, let me know.

Okay, particulars for day 1 and day 2 in the life of your new patients.

Do you intend to adjust on the first visit? Most practice growth gurus say no. And I see the logic in that. If you do adjust on the first visit, there are three things that can happen:

1) The patient gets better, and stops care, and tells nobody because their result was no more than they expected.

2) The patient experiences no change, gets frustrated, blames Chiropractic for not working, stops care, and tells all their friends that Chiropractic doesn't work.

3) The patient gets worse, blames you and Chiropractic, stops care, and tells all their friends that you hurt them.

All three responses are due lack of time in which

to build a relationship, and to teach them about how Chiropractic care works, and why it's important to stick with it.

So - don't adjust on the first visit. (With all of that said, I have to tell you that I always adjust on the first visit. It's a mental hurdle I just haven't gotten past. In 30 years of practice!)

A rough overview of how I do my first visits is:

1st Visit – The patient fills out their intake paperwork, receives a brief tour of the office and brief introduction to the staff, has their pre-care consultation, which includes a brief outline on what 100% health is (feeling well, functioning well, no degenerative stuff like arthritis, diabetes, heart disease, etc.), the six ingredients of health, how misalignments of the spine impact health, and my recommendations for exam and x-rays. Then we perform the exam and x-rays, have the patient watch a video on Chiropractic while the films are being processed (we use the Pro-adjuster, so we use their video), and then do the first adjustment with a VERY brief overview of what I found in the exam. We finish the first visit by giving them recommendations for icing and any restrictions on activities that are appropriate, and set their next appointment within 2 days. (Whew! See why this will be hard to convey by e-mail? That description didn't even include the scripts or exam that we do. I can get to that eventually if you want that much detail.)

2nd Visit – The patient seees a short video on Chiropractic (we use the Renaissance video on Report of Findings.) I then go over their films, go over all my recommendations, adjust them, and set appointments for their new patient workshop, progress exam (usually in 3 months), and next appointment.

3rd Visit – We give the patient their second adjustment, briefly review their ROF, and make sure they are scheduled for a new patient workshop.

Workshop – We have each new patient attend a group class - a one hour workshop called "Reservoir of Health" where we interactively teach practical ways to address the six areas of health, and teach them their prescribed exercises. Attendance at this workshop is as mandatory as I can make it without actually dismissing them from care for not attending. One incentive is that we teach them their rehabilitative exercises at that workshop. I have found that attendance at a workshop makes patients more compliant with recommendations, helps them recover stability in their health faster, and stimulates referrals.

Okay. That's enough for this time.
I'll try to figure out how to send you:
- My new patient paperwork
- Report of findings papers
- Exam forms
-A copy of the Reservoir of Health workshop power

point

Scripts are tougher. I'll see if I have a copy of them somewhere. I'd hate to have to type them all out.

Blessings,

Dr. Chuck Roost

-----Original Message-----
From: Dr. Storyl storylchiro@mail.com
To: healthyus@mail.com
Sent: Fri, Aug 21, 2009 3:24 pm
Subject: Re: hello

Hi Dr. Roost,

Thank you for the concepts you passed on in your last e-mail. I am very appreciative of them and feel they will benefit me greatly if I utilize the advice.

In regards to my practice situation, it will likely be from scratch--I have a few spaces I am seriously considering; but I am also looking for doctors interested in selling their existing practice--there is one in particular I have been talking with. So, it is still not certain yet which route will be taken.

In regards to which of your resources I feel would be best to start with, perhaps patient forms and scripts used for initial visits (Day 1 and Day 2).

Well, I suppose for now any forms and/or scripted conversations that you/staff have with the patients initially (laying the foundation) would be a wonderful place to start. Thanks again!

Because of Christ,

Dr. Storyl

FOUR – 4

-----Original Message-----
From: Dr. Storyl storylchiro@mail.com
To: healthyus@mail.com
Sent: Fri, Aug 28, 2009 9:27 am
Subject: Thanks

Good morning Dr. Roost!

I just wanted to let you know that I received your mail package yesterday. I didn't get home until late... and actually have barely perused it thus far. But I am eager to look through it carefully and am just truly thankful for your willingness to send along all of your office paperwork. It encourages me greatly as I journey along.

It has been a neat week. I have most likely determined my office site. And we have estimated total build out needed (which isn't much)--mainly it's lead drywall in the x-ray room, some carpet changes and a new coat of paint--that's a gift from the Lord for sure! And I found great deals on some office furniture on Craig's List. I am spending a lot less than I allotted for purchases--so that also has been a source of praise. I sense so powerfully God's hand in this whole process, and His tangible assurance that He is holding my hand through it all; that it's all for His glory and I'm merely a vessel to testify to His greatness. So, the pressure is lifted when I truly live in line with that truth. It's one I must return to daily... and sometimes often throughout the day. But those are some of the big things happening.

I'm now just looking into joining civic groups, the

Chamber, and other ways to network and meet people in the community. Do you have any business exposure ideas that have worked well for you? Two other things I am trying to reach a decision on soon that I wanted to ask you about: 1- what type of a business entity are you? I'm debating between an LLC and S Corp. I need to talk with an accountant, I know; they will likely offer me the best advice there. and 2- what type of computer software do you use? I'm hoping to establish the practice as a cash practice, and not directly bill insurance companies. But I'd still like software that provides good notes and coding so that patients can send in their superbills for reimbursement.

Well, thank you so much for the materials, again. I'll touch base with you after I look them over. I just wanted to let you know that I received them. May you have a great weekend. And I look forward to talking to you again soon!

For God's glory,

Dr. S

Five - 5

Dr. Storyl,

Great report! Glad you're making headway. Let me know if the packet of papers is confusing. I wasn't sure how to put it together without pointing out each piece and talking it over. But it should be of some help. Feel free to use them, change them, or pitch them.

Okay –

- **Legal organization**. First off, know that I am no expert. I strongly recommend you get legal and accounting help from professionals. Develop a team of these whom you trust and to whom you can go to for answers.

I am organized legally as a "sole proprietor". I understand that there are reasons for having legal entities (LLC, PLC, etc.) between your personal stuff and your practice entity, but I've not ever had any reason to take on the extra expense and complications of doing an LLC or an S Corp for the practice. I do have an LLC to hold some of my property. My colleague (an independent contractor in my office) is organized under an S Corp and dislikes the paperwork and expense and insurance tangles he encounters. I tend to take the simple way, perhaps to the point of leaving some of my 'stuff' exposed to risk. You might want to get several other inputs on this one. (By the way, and for what it is worth, my dad is a CPA, and he is very content with the way I've done this for the last 30 years.)

- **Computer software** - we use Thomas by Genius for front desk. It's the old version (DOS based rather than windows based) and thus won't do Electronic Records. EHR is eventually going to be required, so I purchased Pro-Soft, and regret it. It's a great, thorough program, but it's overkill for what we can do with our narrow scope here in Michigan. If I were starting new, I'd do either Chiro Touch or the newer version of Thomas, and do as much as possible with patients checking themselves in and out, and start with EHR right off. (Side Note: this information has already become outdated, we've upgraded to E Thomas. The transition was a good bit of work, but then new system works fine. It is worth researching this carefully for your own use in your state.)

- **Marketing** - Always look for people, faces, individuals and businesses to network with. Always ask what is happening in people's lives, showing genuine interest in their life, and at the same time be ready to share:
  - What you are doing
  - What makes you different from the other Chiropractors in your community
  - How you can help
  - How they can get involved in your office

This requires a couple handy tools prepared before you need them:
  - A business card ALWAYS at hand - preferably with something unique on it - perhaps your snappy mission or vision statement.
  - A USP (Unique Selling Point) - have three talks comfortably memorized, and always be ready to share the appropriate one:
1) a 30 second, 2 sentence blurb about your practice
2) a 3 minute commercial that you could share on an elevator ride - same talk, just more depth
3) a 20 minute talk on Chiropractic, health and how

you can help people – preferably complete with power point or visual aids of some sort

- An awareness of opportunities. This is your mindset when you pay for gas, when you go to church (though with tact and subtlety) at the grocery store - everywhere, all day long.

- A deep belief that you have something wonderful to share with people. No apologies, no shame - you are holding the keys to better health for every person you meet. Give them the chance to come along.

Enough for today?

Blessings,

Dr. R

Okay, you get the idea. The move from graduation to practice is a maze of options, decisions, balancing pros and cons, and compromise. Less compromise between what you want and what you actually get is better, but by the time you balance your budget against the cost of equipment, and balance the hours you need staff against the availability of potential employees, and balance a highly visible location against the availability and price of office space, there is going to be some give and take along the way.

And of course, in order to live a life of lasting value and internal consistency, all of these decisions must be run through the filter of our initial question of "What will motivate my life – self, or Christ?" How we obtain new patients, how we interact with them, how we bill insurance, what services we offer – all of these factors of running a practice will be impacted by our deepest motivation – our purpose. That is why being at peace with your purpose statement is so important. (See introduction discussion on mission statement.)

Now let's dig into the nuts and bolts of practice building some more. In these chapters we will look at several of the topics we touched on in my letters to Dr. Storyl, as well as others that can make your practice function as smoothly as a perfectly aligned atlas.

Again, each of these aspects of practice management and practice development will be addressed through the lens of a key question, starting with -

Chapter 7

Practice Management

Question Number Seven: How do we maximize our income generating potential while also staying true to our call to meet needs and point people toward God?

As we Chiropractors forge our way through our professional lives, we each face one big question. 'How do we balance our professional calling against the call to eternally and significantly impact our circle of influence (our family, patients, etc.)?' 'How do we walk the line between success and significance?' Perhaps the best question to consider as we enter this next section is Question Number Seven, 'How do we maximize our income generating potential while also staying true to our call to meeting needs and pointing people toward God?'

Okay, those were three big questions. But the answer to each is just a slightly different view of the same answer.

As to the first question, balancing our profession with our eternal calling requires regular, repetitive, consistent reminders of why we are doing what we are doing. Without these reminders, we tend to drift off purpose into simple, mechanical, business mode, missing opportunities to sow eternal seed. We are blessed in our profession to have a willing audience of people who seek us out for advice. If we keep our mission statement in mind, it is a small step from assisting them with their physical goals (a task for which we are imminently suited in Chiropractic) to encouraging them to seek God in their journey through life (a task for which we should be aptly prepared if we take our Bible seriously). Certainly we, of all health care professionals, can understand how the spiritual impacts the physical, and can offer direction and advice in both arenas. This is another way of saying, work on your own statement of purpose, and then work on making all you do support that purpose.

It takes spiritual discernment to know how much to say and when. But God has given us His Holy Spirit to direct us with that. What a great platform Chiropractic is from which to really help people find wholeness, health, and to meet their full potential. The credibility of a health care professional linked to a profession which so easily addresses the physical and the spiritual forms a place to stand, from which people hear – really hear – what we are saying.

The second question - walking the line between success and significance – is much the same. We are each given a finite number of hours in our lives. My calculations peg that number at 655,200 hours. That's the number of hours in a 75 year life span. It's not that huge of a number when you consider that it's all you get. It is sobering to me to realize that God has given us the responsibility to use them however we desire. You and I get to choose how we spend them – every one of them. We get them, we use them, we trade them just like cash, for something.

The scary part of this is that there are no refunds. No returns. No exchanges. Every day, 24 of them disappear. Every year – 8736 of them gone forever. Once spent, they are gone forever. By the time we graduate from Chiropractic school we have already spent 210,000 of them, one third of our lifetime allotment of hours!

As Gregg Hurwitz put it, "At some point in life, each person realizes that the roller coaster of life won't last forever. We suddenly sense that we've done the two loops, all that is left is the corkscrew, and then the ride is over."

To make this topic even more compelling, understand that we really don't get 24 hours a day to spend as we like. In reality, most of our hours are used up in non-discretionary spending – a fancy term for 'you've got to use them in certain ways.'

Of each 24 hour chunk of time, you use 8 of them for sleeping. Then you use 8 more of them for either work or school. That leaves only 8 hours each day to use as you please.

Of that remaining 8 hours you will use 2 of them for eating, 2 hours for bathing, washing clothes and personal upkeep, and yet another hour for the routine maintenance of life – buying gas for your car, grocery shopping, changing the oil, mowing the lawn, shoveling snow, and the other things you can't live without doing – at least not without making your spouse, neighbors or stomach upset with you.

We could argue over some of the details of this list – I can hear it now – "What about weekends?" or, " I only work 38 hours a week!", or, "I need only 7 hours of sleep each night!" Well, take the time to honestly work through your schedule, and you will find that, by the time you figure in travel time, study time, naps, and all the other minutia of keeping your life going, it is pretty close to these numbers. What it boils down to is that we each have only about 3 hours of discretionary time each day. That's it. 3 hours each day with which we can do whatever we want.

So what do you do with them? Don't tell me what you think you should do with them. Don't tell me what you'd like to do with them. Look back over your last week and tell me what you actually did with them.

Television? Working out? Going to church? Reading the paper? Volunteering at a homeless shelter? Playing ball with the guys? Fishing? Going to a movie? Washing your new car? Playing with your kids? Walking and talking with your spouse? Time on facebook? Planning your vacation? Some alone time? Chatting with a neighbor? Working a crossword puzzle?

You probably read that list and mentally put the items on a spectrum of what is a wise use of time, and what is a waste. I know I did as I wrote it out. But none of them is particularly bad, none overtly sinful. Still, when you realize that you've only got 3 to use, that those 3 hours are, at the same time, both discretionary and irreplaceable – it makes it a lot more compelling to choose wisely. You can do anything you want with them – you get to choose.

I would suggest you choose wisely, for those 3 hours daily are the only thing over which you really have control– how you spend your three hours. So think through your daily schedule. How are you spending your irreplaceable hours? Are you swapping them for entertainment, money, and self? Or are you investing them in loving people and knowing God better?

And then, the final question – the question of maximizing the overall potential of our professional lives – particularly in terms of building a healthy, thriving, productive practice. How do you build a healthy practice in an integrous, productive fashion? This is a question that is extremely simple - and mind bogglingly complex. Simple, in that there are only four factors that impact it. Complex, in that implementing those four fundamental factors, the four factors that impact practice growth, in light of your unique talents and skills and personalities, will demand all of your wisdom and discernment, and all of your ability to tap into the leading of the Holy Spirit.

The four factors of business growth?

- **New business** – attracting new patients.
- **Repeat business** – retaining existing patients for reasons that are in their best interest
- **Increased back end business** – offering additional services that your patients want and need
- **Internal controls** – limiting expenses without

sacrificing quality, and training of yourself and
your staff.

It really is that simple. In fact it sounds too simple.
Four easy pieces of business growth. But each of these
factors is a topic that will require focus and skill to
master. I'm no practice management guru, but I would
like to take the next few chapters to develop each of
these imperative factors a little bit.

Before diving into the four facets, we must first
come to grips with the idea that it is okay for a Christian
to succeed in business. Having money is not evil. In
fact, while God can impact people's lives through poor
people who love Him and share that love with others,
it is also a fact that it is easier to help the widows, feed
the poor, and use a skill set like yours to impact many
people when you have ample money, than it is when
creditors are knocking on the door. Used wisely, money
is a powerful tool in spreading the gospel. If you cannot
be at peace with this concept, you will likely be plagued
with subconscious counter-intent that will cripple your
ability to run a successful practice. Take some time to
resolve this dilemma in your heart, because a "poverty
complex" is going to bind you and hold you back as you
attempt to maximize the impact of your career for the
kingdom.

Just as we only have 3 discretionary hours each day
to trade for eternally significant return, we also only have
a finite number of weeks to use in our practices. This is
subtly different from the hours per day figure, because

the weeks we will use in our career are a measure of how many lives we can touch for the kingdom. This is a healthy way of looking at the people whom God entrusts to us to plant seeds and point toward Him.

I did the math for myself and found that starting from today, if I practice until I'm 80 years old, I have only 1443 weeks left of practice. That's not a lot of weeks left with which to invest time and love into people who enter my practice.

Given a certain, less-than-infinite number of weeks left in your professional life, you can use them up in only two basic philosophies of practice. You can see less patients, but spend more time impacting them. Or you can see more patients and spend less time with each one. Either is fine as long as you recognize that the time you spend with each patient is an opportunity to impact them for physical and spiritual wellness. With your own unique personality, skills, and abilities, how do you best interact with people? When you understand this, you can then design your practice style around those parameters.

It is best to determine which of the above formats you wish to form your practice around so that you can intentionally build your practice protocols to fit.

Another way to look at your case management is to determine what sort of results you desire to aim your care and recommendations at. One style is to work with only symptomatic patients, and focus on relief of symptoms in your recommendations for care. This leads to a shorter length of treatment, and requires a higher number of new patients to keep the practice busy. A second philosophy of results based care is maximizing health potential, where symptoms are secondary to (though they still tend to abate with) improving spinal function, motion, or biomechanics. Aiming beyond symptoms to function improvement for a care plan will require a longer care plan for each patient, and this requires a lower number of new patients to maintain practice viability.

Thus, the results you aim for will determine the number of patients you interact with in your career, and how long you have them under care. Remember that you have only a finite number of weeks to use in your career. Aim to impact as many people for the kingdom as possible, as deeply as possible, with the months and years you have remaining in practice.

For now, let's remember:

-      Seek first to know your purpose, then filter all of your decisions through that mission statement
-      Remember that you are the steward of your hours and minutes
-      Discipline yourself to take time to master each of the four factors of a healthy business

And ask yourself, "How do I maximize my income generating potential while also maximizing my call to meet needs and point people toward God?" This is a part of trading your hours wisely, and using your practice life-span with eternity in mind.

Chapter 8

The First Factor Of Business Success – New Business

Question Number Eight – What are you willing to trade for a new patient?

In the last chapter we asked a key question, a question that addresses the importance of trading our minutes wisely as we go through a day, (a day, if you recall that only allots us about 3 discretionary hours). We spoke about the importance of trading our minutes for significant return – loving God and loving people. We also looked at the fact that our years here, and the years we will have in practice, are not infinite. You can do the math for yourself. Subtract your current age from your expected retirement age, or from your potential lifespan if you plan to work past "normal" retirement right up to the day you die. Multiply that number by 52. That is the number of weeks you have left in which to impact your world through your career for Christ and His kingdom. That number is 1388 for me – if I practice until I'm 80. Sobering, isn't it?

We also introduced the four simple factors necessary to make a business grow.

Do you remember what they are?

- **New business** – attracting new patients.
- **Repeat business** – retaining existing patients

for reasons that are in their best interest
- **Increased back end business** – offering additional services that our patients want and need
- **Internal controls** – limiting expenses without sacrificing quality, and training of ourselves and our staff

As you think about what style of care you want to offer your patients (acute care, wellness care, high volume practice, or some combination of these), you will be formulating how you will do examinations, what x-rays you may order, what your recommendations for care will look like, and how long you will keep a patient under your care. But in any case, it is imperative to be able to attract as many new patients as you need to fuel your practice.

Therefore in this chapter we will focus on the first factor. Finding new business. And since this is not a format for the great detail this topic can contain, we will try to keep it simple. New business in any field of business is critical, and no less so in a Chiropractic practice. It is the life-blood of a healthy practice. In fact, this is perhaps even more so in Chiropractic than in many businesses because we are so good at what we do. We get sick people better, and therefore, people drop out of our practices. Due to this, we must have new patients on a regular basis to stay fluid.

And don't kid yourself, patients will drop out of your practice. Some of even your highly relational, deeply committed doctor/patient relationships will come to an end. In fact, other than your mother, and perhaps your spouse, patients always find a reason to drift away eventually. I occasionally look back at some of the best patient relationships I've had and wonder, "What ever happened to them?" Patients move away, they lose their insurance, they get married to a spouse who likes their own DC better, they pass away, they buy a car that uses up their "Chiro-dollars", they visit their MD who tells them a Chiropractic adjustment may cause a stroke and they believe him. For any of a hundred reasons, people will drop out of your practice. That means that they have to be replaced.

There are two ways to bring in new business. Internal marketing and external marketing. It would be nice if you did not need to lower yourself to "marketing" or sales, but both are critical, and you must pay intentional attention to both, or you will see your practices, and your finances, and your ministry in your practices suffer. If you have a hard time accepting the fact that you must market and sell, try looking on it as a process of education, teaching people how they can experience better health. That is what we do, like it or not. You are a teacher, an educator. And to stay in business, you will need to do this with excellence, skill, and passion.

Internal marketing includes such things as: news letters to your existing patients, making sure your patients are pleased with your level of service, and asking for referrals. When you put intention and energy into these three areas, you will find your practice growing in astonishing ways. But it does take discipline – to do a quality news letter on a consistent basis, to exceed our patients' expectations, to educate your patients on each and every visit, and to ask for referrals in a low pressure way, but on a consistent, pre-planned time table. Discipline yourself to learn how to do each of these tasks in an efficient, high quality, selfless way. Also, train your staff to help. They can listen to patients talk, and when the patient speaks of how well they are doing, tell them to tell others about your office.

External marketing includes: yellow pages ads, road-side visibility, spinal screenings, outside speaking engagements, expos, handing out business cards, networking, web site presence, search engine optimization, phone campaigns, and so on. The challenge is that all of these are important, but none of us likes to do all of them. You will find that you have your own strong areas, and your own weak areas. But that is no excuse for avoiding them. You must do **all of them** or you will develop a weak link in the chain of events that leads to a new patient coming into your office.

Envision a table with legs holding it up. Each leg is a distinct marketing tool.

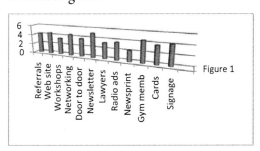

Figure 1

The more legs you have holding the table up, the more stable the table. The more avenues of ingress into your practice, the healthier your practice will be. At the same time, if one avenue of new business dries up (your web site crashes, your sign out front falls over, you lose your yellow pages ad, etc.) there are still multiple pipelines of new patients into your practice.

Sit down in a quiet place. Set up a calendar of committed times to work on each of the internal and external events. Study, or find a teacher to help you to become proficient at each one. And do them. Assign a staff member (or your spouse) to hold you accountable to do them, and do them. If you have the financial flexibility, hire a person to do these marketing efforts for you. You will still need to work along side them to keep them focused, but a staff person whose job description includes marketing tasks will add energy to the new patient acquisition process.

What will you trade to obtain a new patient? The question is complex, because it forces the issues of "return on investment" as well as the level of professionalism you will keep in your marketing efforts. It is a question that is well worth thinking over more than just once.

Set a goal for your ideal number of new patients per week. You can do this by working backward from your desired net income, and dividing that by your "case average" statistic. (See Chapter 11 discussion on statistics.) But set your New Patient goal high enough that you don't feel pressure to "sell" or "close" or even keep every potential new patient who walk in your front door. (See Chapter 3, page 9 discussion on quality new patients.)

The result of internal and external marketing, or patient education, is new patients – one of the four most important keys to a healthy, productive, significant, prosperous practice. Don't waste your years of experience, nor your talents, nor your education, nor your potential, nor your calling, by settling for a mediocre practice. Focus, learn, stretch yourself – and build a healthy, productive practice that impacts many patients with better health, and points each of them toward a deeper relationship with their Creator.

Chapter 9

The Second Simple Factor Of Business Success - Repeat Business

Question Number Nine: Who needs your care anyway?

We're on a roll. We have been speaking about the importance of trading our minutes for significant return – loving God and loving people. We've also begun to dissect the four factors necessary to make a business grow, and we've discussed the first factor – New Business.

Our discussion of internal and external marketing covered specific tools for attracting new patients to our offices. We also mentioned the importance of becoming experts in presenting these tools – communication, writing, networking, asking for referrals, and so on. Now let's dig into some ways to maximize repeat business.

Of the four factors, **New business, Repeat business, Increased back end business, and Internal controls,** repeat business seems to be the hardest to master. It brings into play many factors, including educating your new patients, and balancing our recommendations against the tendency of patients to desire to get the least care they can. We all know what every patient's main goal is – to get out of your office. And who can blame them? As nice as you are, it still costs the patient time and money to be there. Would you spend 20 minutes and forty dollars to spend five minutes with you?

The key here is to meet your patients' need for ongoing care, including rehabilitation and maintenance care, and that requires mastery of two areas. One – you must understand, for yourself, and at a deep level, why it is important to stay under regular Chiropractic care. And two – you must become an expert in teaching them the importance of Chiropractic care beyond the point at which they feel better.

We all know what drives 99% of our patients into our front door to begin with – pain. Usually back pain, headaches, neck pain, or some variation on these musculo-skeletal attention-getters. This is good and bad for us as business owners. Pain brings them to us, so we have an opportunity to educate them about the real meaning of health. But when the pain is gone – they are too, unless we have done a good job of communicating the truth to them.

What is the message you must get across? That health is made up of more than simply feeling good. There is also functioning well – including motion, activities of daily living, good sleep, immune function, digestion, quality of life, and the rest of 100% function. And there is also degeneration – and making sure it doesn't happen any sooner than it absolutely has to. Regular adjustments maximize all of these factors, and there are many research articles that support these claims.

The extent to which you get that truth into their heads and hearts will determine whether your patients will follow through with a maintenance adjustment plan. And it is far more than business, it is life! Both length and quality of life improve with regular, quality Chiropractic care. When the spine functions well, it allows maximum fulfillment of purpose. One of the tenets of Chiropractic lifestyle is to assist people in doing all they were put here to do. It allows for healthy relationships – for lack of function saps emotions and energy right out of relationships. This is not kids' stuff, it is IMPORTANT.

There are three main points during the new patient cycle at which you have maximum opportunity to teach – your consultation, your report of findings, and your new patient workshop.

Do the work ahead of time to develop solid talks on each of these, and then reach the level of unconscious competence in presenting them. The consultation and report of findings should each take about five minutes – plus time for questions. The new patient workshop should last about 45 minutes, and is best if supported with a visual component, such as power point, and props, such as a dry spine, and other object lessons that help you make your point.

The main goal of the consultation is to make sure the new patient knows that you understand their problem, and that you have the answer. The main outcome for each report of findings is that the patient understand your plan and agree to it. And the outcome for the new patient workshop is that they gain tools to help themselves and that they desire to refer others to you.

If you would like a copy of our version of any of these three patient encounters, contact me.

Then, use every office visit as an opportunity to reinforce each component that you have already taught:

- We understand your problem
- We can help
- You are (or are not) following our recommendations as you agreed during your report
    - o Adjustment schedule
    - o Supportive measures such as orthotics, nutritional supplements, massage, etc.
- Here are the things you can do to be healthier
    - o Nutrition components – water intake, diet
    - o Exercise components – spinal rehab, core stability, cardio work, resistance training, and balance training
    - o Proper rest
- Position and support
    - o Stress management
    - o Spiritual issues
    - o Are you doing them?
    - o How can we help you do them more consistently?
    - o Develop a series of topics to teach – one minute at each office visit on 12 topics of health. Then do one of them with every visit.

Doctors – teach your patients how to be healthy. It is a major part of the mission of your life, given to you by God when He led you into your great profession. Work out this mission with fear and trembling. Don't coast through it – reach as many people as you can, and as well as you can. Use all your skills, wisdom, discernment, and communication tools, and reach them. People are literally dying for lack of what you have to offer.

Every patient that leaves your practice on the basis of merely 'feeling better' is walking deeper into degeneration, further into assuming that the level of function they have is good enough, and further down the slope of accepting that they have no other choice other than getting weaker and stiffer with age. They will go on with the false belief that they need more medications for every new malady they encounter until the day they die. That is just not good enough!

Who needs your care? Only those who have a spine and a life to live well.

Chapter 10

The Third Factor Of Business Success – Back End Business

Question Number Ten: Is it ethical to sell 'stuff' to patients?

We continue to unpack the four simple factors necessary to make a business grow. If you've had time to implement these ideas, you have already seen your practice take on new life – growing in numbers, in income, in enthusiasm, in lowered stress, and in impact on patients' lives.

We are moving on. We are in the middle of four chapters on building a thriving business with a Christian ethic and eternal mindset. So keep in mind that, while a healthy business is important, it is imperative to base our business on the two most important foci in the world – loving God and loving people. This is all integral to living above the level of the tree tops.

The four factors important to building a healthy business?

- **New business** – attracting new patients.
- **Repeat business** – retaining existing patients for reasons that are in their best interest
- **Increased back end business** – offering additional services that our patients want and need

- **Internal controls** – limiting expenses without sacrificing quality, and training of ourselves and our staff

We've already developed ways to find new patients, and how to ethically maximize repeat business. Now let's dive into the third area of a healthy business – "Back End Business".

The term sounds negative, but it simply means finding services or goods that your current patients need, and then providing those services to your patients in a way, and at a price, that builds a win-win situation for you and the patient. Remember, these are things that they already need to implement into their life in order to either return to health or to stay healthy, and they are things they would end up buying somewhere anyway, and probably from someone with less of their best interest at heart.

You are seeking to fill a need without selling people things they don't need. We are simply attempting to meet a need without creating an artificial need. There is a clear line between:

- helping people realize how to be healthier and offering them a way to achieve that goal, and
- convincing people to purchase goods and services they really don't need.

So, what can we offer that will contribute to either a longer life or a better life? First of all, education. We are teachers, after all. So let's teach. Teach them about the six essential building blocks to better health, which include:

- Nutrition
- Rest
- Exercise
- Stress Management
- Spiritual Health
- Spine Health

Become an expert in each of these areas of health maintenance, then become an expert in communicating their importance. Teach them in small pieces as well as longer sessions. Teach them off the cuff and in formal classes. Teach them when they ask questions, and teach them as questions come to your mind that they should have asked but didn't. Teach them during every visit, and teach your staff to teach them.

As your patients understand the importance of each of these areas of maximum health, give them opportunities to meet those needs. Research, find, and offer high quality goods and services that meet those needs.

What kinds of goods and services you elect to provide will vary depending on your state laws, your expertise, and your interests. But the options are very diverse.

Provide a line of nutritional supplements that are 'bioavailable' and effective. Provide ways to address posture and support in sleep. Offer programs that assist them in stabilizing the corrections you make to their spine with orthotics, or simple exercise equipment such as stability balls, DVDs on healthy exercise, foam rollers, and elastic resistance bands. Provide avenues to exercise in safe ways that strengthen the spine as well as the heart, lungs, joints and muscles. Show practical ways to lower stress and manage it. Instruct people on why it is important to take proper care of the spine, and then offer affordable ways to stay on a maintenance plan of spinal adjustments. Offer healthy alternatives for snacks and drinks. And whenever the opportunity shows itself, share the path toward Christ with discernment and grace.

To provide these services requires some research on your part. You want to be able to tell people that you are offering high quality goods and services that you would use yourself, and that you would recommend to your own family. In fact, in our office, we provide all of these products to our staff at reduced rates, and give some of them free to staff. That's how highly we value their impact on our own health. I decided that if I think these products make a difference in health, and I want my staff to be healthy, I'll invest in them in this way. It's simply a part of their employment benefit package.

When you consider the question of integrity and sales in your office, keep your motivation straight, and you'll have no trouble staying on the high road. There is nothing wrong with making a fair profit from meeting a true need. All we are doing is teaching truth and giving opportunities for people to have a better life. Just be sure to do it with excellence, and with integrity.

Chapter 11

The Fourth Factor Of Business Success – Internal Controls

Question Number Eleven: How well do you know the condition of your business?

Let's talk about internal controls. This is a broad topic in reference to growing a business, so we will address only three areas within it. First we will turn our attention to limiting expenses. I have to admit that this is a weak area for me in my practice. In the attempt to provide my patients with an excellent experience every time they enter our office, I may go too far. We serve fresh coffee, hot tea and filtered water in the waiting room. We have snacks and newer reading materials available. The rest room is as clean and comfortable as the bathrooms in my home. (Without the shower. We haven't gone that far. Yet.)

Our staff members are friendly, attentive, and good at what they do. We aim to have each patient wait 5 minutes or less. We have answers ready for any question that is likely to be asked. Records are ready for patient treatment before the patient enters the office. We offer all the latest diagnostic and treatment equipment that we can afford to provide. We strive for excellence, and people enjoy coming to our office. Our goal is to exceed their expectations, and we accomplish this almost every time. A good motto to work with is, "Promise less than you can deliver, and deliver more than you promise." Don't promise a new client the moon, but do all you can to provide it. Provide a "Wow!" encounter, and patients will go away talking about their great experience in your office.

But it is possible to get carried away with this, too. Many of us love an excuse to spend money. Expenses can get out of hand if they are not watched carefully, and the trend has to be reigned in a bit. Review this on occasion. Have a trusted advisor look at it once in awhile. We want to have a sharp image, but balanced with reasonable cost.

Another important piece of cost control is staffing, including numbers of staff, pay rates, and bonus systems. There are many state laws that address this topic, but here are a few pointers that have worked for me.

-    Many suggest you need one staff person for every 100 patient visits you see each week. I have found that this is too few. With that ratio, things don't get done that should get done. Statistics get set aside for 'when we have time', patient services lag, waiting room time grows longer, billing gets confused, filing gets done wrong or not at all. Be sure you have enough staff that you, the doctor, have time to do the planning, marketing and strategizing that allow for continued practice growth.

-    If you want to attract and keep quality staff you will have to pay well over minimum wage. And it helps to offer some benefits. It does not have to be a full health and retirement package for every staff member, but your key staff are worth these extras if you expect them to stay past the next 'better offer' that comes their way.

- I don't offer paid sick days. Why reward sickness? On the other hand, you may find it helpful to let them earn paid vacation time. Other perqs can include free care for them and their immediate family, nutritional supplements, and paid holidays.

- We bonus based on office production. When collections go up, we pay a bonus rate per hour over their base hourly rate. This makes it 'worth it' for them to work harder.

- We also do 'games' in which there may be cash prizes. If the doctor forgets to change the headrest paper, he puts a dollar into a kitty that the staff draws for at the next staff meeting. Enlisting patients in referral programs or office contests can earn cash bonuses as well.

Next, let's discuss in-office statistics. Statistics can be dry, boring, time-consuming data on a spread sheet, or they can be a revealing glimpse into the health, the strengths and the weaknesses, of your practice. They can uncover the hidden barriers of your patient flow that are hindering your growth. They can reveal the areas of patient interaction on which you should focus your improvement efforts.

You don't need to keep a whole raft of statistics, just a few will give you great insight into your business. Let me list a few, and what they can tell you, then you can decide which ones you need to keep an eye on.

- **New Patients** (NP) – the number of new patients

per week – tells you how effective your marketing is.

- **Patient Volume** (PV) – the number of patient visits per week – gives you more than just bragging rights, this number will be used to develop other revealing numbers.
- **Money Collected** – the number of dollars collected per week – the IRS will thank you.
- **Patient Retention** (PV divided by NP) – tells you how well you are retaining your New Patients, and how well you are educating them.
- **Case Average** (Money Collected divided by NP) – tells you how much each NP brings into your practice – critical for knowing how effective your marketing must be – how much you can afford to spend on marketing to bring in a new patient.
- **Visit Average** (Money Collected divided by PV) – tells you how efficient your front desk is at collecting your fees.
- **Visit Drop** – the visit number on which each new patient drops out of care – care to guess on which visit most patients drop out of care? You'll be shocked. It's usually visit number two, but check your own stats, and let me know if I'm wrong. Knowing this will help you see where your patient education efforts are weak or failing.

See? Stats can be fun. And sobering. Train a staff member to record and report these to you each week. They will need about an hour each week to produce them. Review your numbers each week, and use them to decide where you need to invest more time and effort inside your practice.

The third facet of this area of business growth is training. And the key to this is not usually outside classes, though those may be helpful at times. The real key to a sharp staff and smooth teamwork is regular staff meetings. We do ours twice a month – without fail. And attendance is mandatory. I buy lunch for the staff just to sweeten the pot, but even without a free lunch, staff meetings are critical to forge a team, to sharpen our skills, and to keep us all doing the right things all the time. Without regular staff meetings, entropy gradually erodes our office policies.

Entropy, the third law of thermodynamics, affects the energy of the universe, the cleanliness of children's bedrooms, and the efforts of staff to stay on task. If allowed to run its normal course, any team will stray from policies, do tasks a bit sloppier every day, and lose focus on how to do what needs to be done in the office. We want our staff sharp and able to do the right task the right way – every time.

So what do we do at staff meetings? First of all we laugh. We tell a joke or two. Next we celebrate. We share victories we have seen in the office and in our families. Then we polish up problem areas that have arisen since the last staff meeting – issues that have come up that are not yet covered in our staff policy manual. Everyone is encouraged to bring their own list of these issues to the table. And then we finish up by covering a major area that every team member has to work on – including things like scripts for new patient phone calls, how to present the report of findings, how to teach exercises that the doctor has prescribed, scripts for posting and scheduling and collections, what paper work has to be done (and how) on the first visit, and so on. We rotate through a series of these types of items from meeting to meeting. Sometimes they seem just a bit repetitive, so we play games with them, letting different staff members teach the topic of the day – and then the rest of us playfully critique how they did. We actually have a lot of fun at these meetings, and as I said above, they serve several very important functions.

In order to grow a healthy business, you must know the condition of its various components. Thus, internal controls. So, tighten the financial screws just a bit – or at least sit down and review where the money is going on occasion. Continue offering an excellent experience to your patients. Watch your statistics and use them to fine tune your business. And keep you and your staff sharp by holding staff meetings – at least twice a month.

Internal controls make up the fourth factor to building a healthy business. Proverbs 27:23 tells us that we are to know well, the "… state of thy flocks, and look well to thy herds." Even Solomon was a proponent of managing with the assistance of statistics. Office statistics allow you to know the condition of your business. But we are not quite done yet. To finish up our discussion of business success we will discuss implementation in the next chapter.

Chapter 12

Implementing The Changes We Need To Make

Question Number Twelve: How are wishes like fishes?

We've covered some ground, eh? We started with aspects of practice that will allow us to practice above the tree tops – five chapters that 'popped the top on', or at least encouraged cogitation over factors that give our lives and our practices a flavor that is tasteful and inviting. We asked key questions that will assist in formulating what your practice will look like when you place Christ first, and put eternal impact on the front burner. Then we discussed the four factors that combine to grow a strong business in a little bit of detail. Again, we asked questions that are designed to get you thinking about what you are doing, what you can do better, and what you might want to add to or trim away from your office protocols and policies in order to get and stay above the level of the tree tops.

There's enough information in those 12 chapters to turn a practice around from a stress to a blessing. From a struggle to a joy. From survival mode to prosperity. From a chore to a ministry. From day after day of drudgery to a fulfilling investment of your time in eternal matters.

Yet there is a missing piece or two. For we can get

a lot of new information, and not change or improve a single thing. We can know, and not implement. We can hear and not obey. We can hear and not do. We can feel and not receive. And it is in the implementing, the obedience, doing, and the receiving that we become victorious in life and in practice.

So, as a last thought in this section, consider this – how do we implement the changes that we now realize we must make? How do we go from mere hearers to victorious doers of what we know we need to do?

Certainly we must trust God for the grace to do what we should. At the same time, however, in God's economy, and by the rules of His kingdom, He still sees fit to leave us with our own free will to do or not to do. There is a balance between God doing for us, and us stepping out to do what we know we should do.

But balance is not quite the right word either. There is no 50 – 50 split between our responsibility and God's. It is more of a 100 – 100 partnership. At the same moment, God does it all, and yet leaves a full job for us to do. Thus, He sends us new patients, yet we must build a business. He uses us to heal people in our profession, yet we train, serve with excellence, and teach practical steps to better health. It is not a balance, it is "both, and" – both Him doing all that needs done, and us being responsible stewards and workers.

So what can help us in taking new information and using it to change old habits into new, stronger routines? There are specific steps to turning our goals into healthy routines. Any one of the following steps will improve the odds of making a goal 'stick' as a new habit, but do several of them together, and they work with one another like compounding interest, exponentially impacting the part of our brain that forges new habits. They act as catalysts on one another, each increasing the effect of the others.

Start with a list. I know, we've all made lists before, and left them in our pockets until they turned to lint. I know I once went through a pile of 'stuff' on my desk that was waiting to be filed, and found three old 'to do' lists that held items that still needed to be done well over a year later.

There are a number of reasons why a comprehensive goal setting system works. One of the reasons the idea works is that part of the brain stem called the Reticular Activating System. Goal setting is not mumbo that sends 'vibes' out into the cosmos that turn the universe into your wish bone. It is more real than that by a long shot.

The Reticular Activating System (RAS) is the part of the brain that makes 'front of mind awareness' work for advertisers. It is the part of the brain that makes you suddenly notice all of the other silver Camrys on the road after you buy yours. It is also the part of the brain that will be on the lookout for opportunities to advance your goals step by step as they come your way. Just like the silver Camrys out there, the opportunities were always there, they were just overlooked until you began noticing them. And you can make the RAS work for you by seeding your brain with thoughts, pictures and steps to your goals.

So lists are valid. One study showed that just the act of making a goals list correlated to a 95% improvement in accomplishment. So this is how we begin to turn intentions and wishes into reality.

Make a list of all of the things you want to do, obtain, achieve and accomplish for the rest of your life. I'm serious. This sounds like a huge task, but with one piece of paper you will run out of ideas before you run out of room. This list should be a living document. You can add to it, and you can take items off as your priorities change in the future. Still, write this list in ink – not pencil. These are important items that will help focus your activities for months and years to come.

Right now, put down this book, grab a sheet of paper and a pen, label it your "Master Goals List", and start writing. Stop reading – start writing. Make a list of all the goals you want in your life. As you formulate your list, be sure to think short term and long – what do you want in a month, a year, 10 years? How about leaving long term accomplishments for your family – think 50 and 100 years.

When you start to run out of ideas, start writing again as you think of goals that relate to your job or professional life. What hours do you wish you could work? Would you like to be debt free? How much vacation time do you want each year? Net worth goals? Lowered stress level? A particular promotion, job description or pay rate?

Then work on goals that impact your personal

and family life – vacations, additions to your home, remodeling your home, exercise, rest, health, fitness, nutrition, weight goals, spa services, lessons and skills to gain, sports, personal time and boundaries in your life, education, retirement and inheritance.

How about material goals – a car, boat, jewelry, furniture, a bike. Material goals should never dominate our lives, but they are okay as long as they are kept in balance.

Next, list spiritual goals – prayer time, meditation, teaching, leadership, ministry, fruitfulness, and the heritage you want to build. In what areas of truth do you want to gain wisdom?

Once you have your list written out, put it someplace safe. A place where you can access it and review it once a month. I keep a copy as a file in my computer, and a hard copy in a file near my desk.

Next, take a notebook and label a page for each of your goals. You will need anywhere from 20 to 100 pages, depending on how many goals you wrote out on your Master Goals List. For each goal write down all of the steps that will need to get done for that goal. The steps you write down should be single action items, things you can do in one sitting, or one errand, or one step. These are called your "Goals Worksheets", and again, you will need to write one of these for each of your goals.

For example, if one of your goals is to learn karate, what are the steps you would have to take to do so? Buy a uniform? Find a teacher or school? Make a slot in your schedule for the classes? Get in some sort of shape to be able to take the abuse you're about to incur? Get permission from your spouse? Make sure your insurance is paid up?

Make this list of steps as specific and complete as possible, and remember to make each step a "one step action" – something you can do in one chore. Then determine which of these is the step that needs to be done first, and put it on another list, called your "Next Actions List".

This list should go in your planner, or purse – wherever you can find it when you need to draw another item from it to place on your daily to-do list. No, you do not need to do this entire list each day, but it will serve to remind you of the items that are important to you.

Now, from your Next Actions List, take three items each day, and write them on what we will call your Must Do List. This list will be a daily chore list. It can contain other things you have to do each day, such as your grocery lists, your errands list, people to call, etc. But the key to this list is the three items you choose each day from your Next Actions List. These are the items, single step actions, that will whittle away at your major goals. Your aim is to all three of these items each day. You can imagine how following through on this system will get things done in your life!

So you've got a Master Goals List. You've got a list of Next Actions Steps that are what has to be done next for each goal. You've taken three of those next action steps and placed them on your daily "MUST DO" list.

Good work! You've taken some serious steps toward becoming a serious doer. Right now – already – you have moved way up in the list of those who accomplish things with their lives. I highly commend you.

But do you want to go further? There are a few more secrets that will turn your wishes into goals, and your goals into accomplishments. Come along with me and take another couple of steps. It won't hurt a bit, and you'll find your life a different place in which to live.

Given two people who have changes to implement in their lives, the one with a partner will always come out ahead. Accountability is a powerful tool in getting a person to move away from an unwanted stand still. You've seen it for yourself, I'm sure. Isn't it a lot easier to go to the gym or for a walk if your buddy is waiting for you? It is absolutely true. So go find someone who you can share one of your lists with – your Goals List, your Goals Worksheets, your Next Action Steps list, or your Must Do list. Ask them to call you weekly to ask you how it's going. Only once a week though. More often, and they become your nag to avoid. Less often, and the pressure is to dilute to do any good.

It's been said that "If wishes were fishes, we'd all be wet." Say that out loud once. "If wishes were fishes, we'd all be wet." Sounds kind of neat rolling off your tongue, doesn't it? But, you might ask, what does that have to do with getting life goals done? Well, a goal without a time frame is just a wish, and we've all got enough wishes. Assigning a time frame is a strong component in turning wishes into goals, and goals into accomplishments. So, go back to your Master Goals List and write a date after each goal. When do you want to have each goal done? Write it down.

This is not a high pressure tactic, it's just a matter of brain mechanics and neurophysiology. When you have a due date, the RAS kicks into a higher gear. If the due date passes without accomplishing that goal – no problem. No penalty. Just think it through, cross out the old date, and put a new one in. You still have added overdrive to your ability to find paths and steps to meet your goal. Consciously AND subconsciously you are seeking and finding ways to achieve your goals.

Looking at your Next Actions List, you will notice that there is always one item that you do not want to do. You will see it there on your list, you will recognize that doing it will only take a moment, it will result in advancing your goals, you will be happier when it's done. But a part of your brain rebels against the thought of tackling that task, and you will find yourself coming up with the most ludicrous, hare-brained reasons for not doing it.

For me, it is usually a phone call. I hate making phone calls. Sometimes I think e-mail was made entirely for me, simply because I will do almost anything to avoid making phone calls.

But a very good piece of advice is to look at your Next Actions List and select for your Must Do List at least one of those actions that you desperately want to avoid. Then, when you look at your Must Do List, do that item first thing in the morning.

This step takes some real guts. Who wants to select their worst chore on the list and then do it first? Well, I've heard it said that if you eat a live frog first thing in the morning, the rest of your day is going to look pretty peachy in comparison. So do the worst thing first, and you'll see the rest of your action steps moving into the "out basket" of your life faster than you would have ever imagined possible. I heard this tip from a great motivational website, www.simpletruths.com. Check them out to light a renewed fire under your feet.

Another way to look at prioritizing is to rank your Master Goals List in order of significance. You will need to access the wisdom of the Holy Spirit to get this right. But pray about which goals are the ones that will impact eternity most, and put them in order. Then take next action steps for those, and make sure they are consistently on your Must Do List.

Now, with all of this in mind, go back to your Master Goals List. Get your pen again, and add at least two items from each of the four topics for practice growth are on the list.

New Business (Chapter 8) – pick one internal and one external marketing tool and write a goal for implementing them.

Repeat Business (Chapter 9) – improve your consultation, report of findings, or daily education processes.

Back End Business (Chapter 10) – learn how patients can improve their nutrition, exercise, stress management, sleep, or posture – and offer them services or materials to implement them.

Internal Controls (Chapter 11) – plan staff meetings twice a month, and check your overhead on a quarterly basis.

Next pick 5 specific ways to practice above the tree tops and place them on your Master Goals List.

Determine your **purpose and mission** (see Chapter 2, page 7) statement.

Atmosphere (Chapter 2) – how can you improve the first impression you make on new arrivals in your practice?

Integrity (Chapter 3) – where can you increase your transparency and honesty?

Staffing (Chapter 4) – where can you improve your staff's 'buy in' to your office philosophy?

Sharing the gospel (Chapter 5) – at what points in your office routines would it be appropriate to speak up about Christ?

This will give you 13 additional items on your Master Goals List, 13 goals related directly to changing your practice for the better. Use the same steps (Goals Worksheet, Next Action Steps, and Must Do List) that you did for the rest of your goals, and watch your practice and your life transform.

One step at a time you will implement new business protocols that will make you more prosperous, a better physician, and more effective at improving your patients' lives physically, as well as spiritually.

One last suggestion for your Master Goals List. Be sure to include some items that are good for you personally – even though you don't really want to make them part of your life. Here is a list of goals that I think each of us should have in our sights, though they are not usually items that people think of right away for their list.

Add to your list, if they are not already there:

- Date your spouse on a regular basis
- Visit your parents
- Find a mentor for yourself
- Find someone to pour yourself into
- Improve your abilities as a communicator
- Be able to share your testimony and the gospel
- Know your purpose and mission statement
- Volunteer time with those in prison, those shut away from the rest of the world, those without parents, and/or the poor

These goals make life a better place for you and for others. Winston Churchill said, "We make a living by what we get, but we make a life by what we give." Be sure a balanced portion of your life is giving – giving to relationships and giving to the benefit of others.

So implementation is that simple. Plan. Write down the changes you need to make. Put the steps into a system like the Must Do List. Get an accountability partner. Get the changes into your regular systems and routines. Don't let your wishes be like fishes – as common as water. Make your wishes into goals, and your goals into accomplishments that will build a life full of eternal meaning. Leave more than memories behind you. Leave a heritage.

I will look forward to celebrating the lives you touched – more lives than you can now imagine – in deeper ways than you now see. It's your calling. It's how you can invest your minutes and hours in significant ways. It is living above the level of the tree tops.

Section 3 – Healing At a Higher Level

W e've asked and discussed and sorted through 12 questions that could easily change your life. Still, questions can be asked and answered without changing a thing in your life. Even more, we could implement a whole bunch of what we've discussed, and still live a whole life without really tapping into the fullness of what God intended for us as His children.

What Jesus did with His death and resurrection is amazing. Consider our release from the penalty of and slavery to sin! Ah! How sweet to know that the death penalty is forgiven! You and I, because we have accepted the gift of forgiveness, are alive, and will live forever in heaven! And because He broke the power of death and sin in His resurrection, we no longer need to sin. We are free to do holy, righteous works with our lives – works that will result in significant, eternal reward, and ever more creative service to God the Father for eternity in heaven.

Now if you have never taken that step of salvation, none of the rest of this book will be of any help to you. The Bible teaches that there is nothing that people can do to earn our way into heaven, so God did it for us out of love. On the one hand, He is so perfect and our sin is so grievous, but on the other hand, His love for us is so vast that He paid the penalty for us.

I like to explain the Bible's plan of salvation as "3 knows and 1 yes".

1) Know that I've sinned. At some point in my life (many points in my own case) I thought, spoke or acted in a manner that was sinful. (Sin is defined as anything in my life that missed the mark of God's holiness and perfection. How's that for an unachievable standard?)

2) Know that there is nothing I can do to erase or make up for that stain on my heart. God's law says that the penalty for any sin is death – eternal separation from God.

3) Know that Jesus, the perfect son, perfect sacrifice, who lived a perfect life, died in my place to pay that penalty.

4) Yes – believing these three truths, I decide that I will accept that payment in my place. The Bible says that with the heart we believe, and with the mouth we speak – verbally affirming that I have taken these four steps. (This may be done aloud but alone, but I encourage a new believer to find another believer to speak this with to help in the next stage – growing your brand new, perfect heart that God places in you when you are saved.)

Once we are saved, however, we are His representatives as spiritually reborn beings in a world bathed in, run by, moved by, and lost in merely material, physical, and logical humanity. We could lead a "good" life and still make "fleshly" decisions, resulting in a life devoid of spiritual or eternal impact.

I submit to you that that is not good enough. Christ did not leave heaven, become a man, live without ever once giving in to sin, get whipped and beaten, bleed and die, and rise again from the dead to have us merely logically think through a slightly better life. Setting aside the power, glory and riches of His godhood, He lived a sinless life, and showed us how to do the same. He empowered us to do what He did, and **"...greater works than these..."**. (John 14:12)

Practicing Chiropractic in a way that allows us to tell people about salvation is great, but He intended more. Building a significant practice in order to bless many people is better than struggling or failing in business, but He granted us much more in His orders to us as His disciples, His representatives here on earth. He left us with orders to take authority over demons and sickness, and to live victoriously over sin, poverty and ineffectiveness. He calls us friends, sons, victors, overcomers and more than mere men.

Some of the key portions of the gospel beyond salvation, purchased at so precious a price, but often overlooked, include salvation, the sending of a helper and His gifts to us, healing, the power of the spoken word, the law of sowing and harvesting, and prayer. In this last section of our book on running a Christian Chiropractic clinic, let's examine how these less-discussed facets of the complete gospel fit into a truly abundant life.

Salvation is, of course, the primary benefit of the gospel. Without it we have nothing, but with it we have access to all of the abundant life that God promises us. Yet, Christ purchased so much more! In leaving His heavenly home, He bought, with His poverty, the right to be rich. With His stripes we were healed. With His return to heaven, He ensured the coming and empowering of the Holy Spirit. With His resurrection, He gave us victory over death. With His victory and His pure life, He gave us the ability to be victorious over sin. With His death, He paid for our sins. With His blood He washed us clean, making us perfectly righteous in God's eyes. In adopting us as His brothers, and thereby making us the Father's children, we are afforded heavenly citizenship and the protection and resources of our new home. The list goes on, but you can see that the full gospel is even more than the wondrous gift of eternal life.

It is difficult to comprehend the mystery that it was to our benefit that Jesus left us and went back to heaven. My mind rebels at this thought, because I would like so much to walk side-by-side and talk face-to-face with the Master as I go through this broken, messed up life. Still, He said it was better that He go, so that He could send us a Helper – the Holy Spirit. In what ways the presence of the Holy Spirit is better than the physical presence of Jesus on the face of the planet is a subject too broad for the substance of this book. We will leave it to another author to explore that. But we must believe it, for Jesus said it. Most of us yawn at the thought that we have the Holy Spirit living in us. Yet Jesus said that that fact is better than walking side by side with Him.

Look at it this way. Most of the nation just saw two people win the fourth largest lottery take in history. How fun for those two! Unfortunately, about 300 million others lost their one dollar 'investment'. Well, if salvation is a lottery ticket that God issues to every person on the planet (It IS His will that ALL come to the saving knowledge of His Son!) (2 Peter 3:9), then every one of us has the winning number. Unfortunately, even though every ticket is a winning ticket, about 90% of the population leaves the ticket in their wallet, never redeeming it for the prize.

Furthermore, once a person turns their ticket in for their salvation, they are given a handful of other tickets – one each for healing, protection, prosperity, wisdom, victory, the leading of the Holy Spirit, and so on. Again, every one of these tickets are winners, but most Christians leave them in their wallets, passing over their opportunity to live in the fullness of the abundant life Christ died to purchase for them.

A few of these other factors: healing, the power of the spoken word, the Law of Sowing and Harvesting, prayer, and the interwoven and underpinning truth of the Law of Jurisdictions – these I would like to address. So in the next 4 chapters let's explore how these facets of the full gospel of Jesus can be used in a Christian clinic and an abundant life.

While these biblical concepts are well documented in the written Word, they have been discussed and debated for nearly 2000 years now. I want to clarify two thoughts here. First, that I do not claim to have the final word on these topics. And second that this is relatively new truth in my own life. I was raised in a church that tended to interpret these factors through a lens of "That was for the early church," thought process. This conviction about the end of the active gifts of the spirit was explained in light of 1 Corinthians 12 where it says that once the perfect has come, the imperfect will be done away – Jesus or the completed written word being the 'perfect', and the "apostolic gifts" being the imperfect.

I am not sure, but I think that it was necessary to explain away the miraculous gifts because those gifts were so rarely seen in experience, even by the leaders – the 'saints' of the church.

Still, though I have come to believe that these gifts are still active, I have had very little experience in practicing them. So these next chapters are a compilation of what I have been learning, and continue to learn, about believing what God says in His Word about living in faith. I hereby testify that I am seeking earnestly the gifts. I want to function at a level that cannot be explained away by any human talent, skill or technique. I would like to have people look at my life and say, "Only God could do that!" I refuse to explain away truth just on the basis of my lack of experiencing them in my own life. I choose to believe that He meant what He said, and to seek to have my experience match that truth hereafter.

So let's dig in. Let's seek the greatest gifts. Let's ask God to use us in ways that we have yet to experience.

It is a matter of biblical record that these are available

to us. We know that they are important, for Jesus paid a dear price for them. Let's not ignore them, but use them as intended for ministry, for the kingdom, for influencing the lives of patients entrusted to us for care.

Chapter 13

The Power of Our Spoken Words

Experience and common sense tell us that our words matter. Even taken as nothing more than a simple mode of communication between two people, our words carry, not just information, but emotional power. (James 3:5) **"Even so the tongue is a little member, and boasteth great things. Behold, how great a matter a little fire kindleth!"** If for no other reason than the impact they have on our relationships, it pays to be aware of our words and the impact they carry. We are admonished to guard every word in Ephesians 4:29, **"Let no corrupt communication proceed out of your mouth, but that which is good to the use of edifying, that it may minister grace unto the hearers."** What a compelling verse – telling us that we can indeed have authority over what comes out of our mouths, and that our words can spread grace to those in range of our speech.

But beyond that, the Bible speaks to the importance and power of our words in an even more powerful manner. Consider the weight of God's words: By His word He created everything that is. (Genesis 1:6, 9, 11, etc.), (Romans 4:17) **"...God, who quickeneth the dead, and calleth those things which be not as though they were."** By His word He wrought the amazing works of the Old Testament.

By His spoken words Christ stilled storms
(Mark 4:36-39) **"And when they had sent away the
multitude, they took him even as he was in the ship.
And there were also with him other little ships. And
there arose a great storm of wind, and the waves beat
into the ship, so that it was now full. And he was in the
hinder part of the ship, asleep on a pillow: and they
awake him, and say unto him, Master, carest thou
not that we perish? And he arose, and rebuked the
wind, and said unto the sea, Peace, be still. And the
wind ceased, and there was a great calm."** Shriveled
an olive tree, commanded demons, raised dead people,
and healed multitudes. And he tells us that by OUR
words, we are saved. (Romans 10:10) **"For with the
heart man believeth unto righteousness; and with
the mouth confession is made unto salvation."** His
very words bring eternal life, (John 6:68), and by His
words we have been authorized to do "…greater things
than these".

Our spoken words flow from what we believe in our
heart (Matthew 15:18) **"…those things which proceed
out of the mouth come forth from the heart; and
they defile the man."** So what we believe is crucial to
our salvation, as well as to what kind of life we lead here
on earth. But the spoken word plays a role in these things
also. In some manner, what we believe is made manifest
in what we speak. God has ordered our world in such a
way that what we truly believe is made to be when we
speak Truth verbally. (Proverbs 18:21) **"Death and life
are in the power of the tongue: and they that love it**

shall eat the fruit thereof."

It follows that with our mouth we can claim everything that God has promised us. One of the ways we are made in His image is that our words have power. Romans 4:17 says that He speaks into existence that which does not exist. And Abraham's faith in God's words changed his world. Just as powerfully, with our mouth, we can erode faith, destroy relationships, and live out all the negativity that Satan would have for us. (Proverbs 13:3) **"He that keepeth his mouth keepeth his life:** *but* **he that openeth wide his lips shall have destruction."** (Proverbs 18:7) **"A fool's mouth is his destruction, and his lips** *are* **the snare of his soul."** Our words offer legal access to either the promises of God, or the attacks of Satan. (James 3:6) **"And the tongue is a fire, a world of iniquity: so is the tongue among our members, that it defileth the whole body, and setteth on fire the course of nature; and it is set on fire of hell."** The Lord God honors His word highly, (Psalm 138:2) and is looking out for it to perform it. (Jeremiah, 1:12).

Look at this passage for a moment: (Matt. 12:34-35) **"O generation of vipers, how can ye, being evil, speak good things? For out of the abundance of the heart the mouth speaketh. A good man out of the good treasure of the heart bringeth forth good things: and an evil man out of the evil treasure bringeth forth evil things."**

Can you see the connection between what we believe in our heart, what comes out of our mouth, and the life that manifests as a result? If you read Job carefully you can see how his belief impacted his security, safety, prosperity and his family. (Job 3:25) **"For the thing which I greatly feared is come upon me, and that which I was afraid of is come unto me."**

You can see it again in (Proverbs 18:20-21) **"A man's belly shall be satisfied with the fruit of his mouth;** *and* **with the increase of his lips shall he be filled. Death and life** *are* **in the power of the tongue: and they that love it shall eat the fruit thereof."** Here, wise Solomon warns us that our spoken words impact our physical experience.

Over and over again scripture reminds us that our words have great impact on our thoughts, our lives, our circumstances, and our health. For instance, (Proverbs 12:18) says, **"There is that speaketh like the piercings of a sword: but the tongue of the wise** *is* **health."**

For some reason God has set up our world in such a way that the physical is subject to the spiritual. And it works in four steps. First, God's Word sets the absolute, foundational truth of a matter. Our belief in that Truth then changes our heart. Next, from our heart (our spiritual belief) flow our words, which in turn change the physical/material world we live in.

Keep in mind that God's word NEVER changes. And we all have to admit that what we see and feel, the things we hear in the world – do change! Things change all the time. Things change from good to bad. Wait a bit and you'll see that eventually bad things change to good. Reports change. The economy changes. Weather changes. Relationships change. Everything around us changes. But God's word never has, never does, and never will.

So one lesson to learn here is to avoid building hope or trust in things that change. In the same way, we should never allow negative emotions to claim us that are caused by negative things around us – they will change, too! They are going to change! Trust God's promises. They never change.

Another view of this principle is that our words, spoken out loud and in faith, force the material world to comply with spiritual truth. (Mark 11:22-23) "**And Jesus answering saith unto them, Have faith in God. For verily I say unto you, That whosoever shall say unto this mountain, Be thou removed, and be thou cast into the sea; and shall not doubt in his heart, but shall believe that those things which he saith shall come to pass; he shall have whatsoever he saith.**"

This is important! Time after time God tells us to guard our mouth. Why is that? It's because our mouths are powerful weapons. With our mouths we are saved. With our faith-filled words we bring curses or blessings. With our verbal agreement with His word we bring His promises to manifestation in our lives.

In fact, we are to be held responsible for EVERY word that we speak! (Matthew 12:36-37) "**But I say unto you, that every idle word that men shall speak, they shall give account thereof in the day of judgment. For by thy words thou shalt be justified, and by thy words thou shalt be condemned.**" Remember

(Ephesians 4:29) **"Let no corrupt communication proceed out of your mouth, but that which is good to the use of edifying, that it may minister grace unto the hearers."** Every word counts. The ones we speak, and the ones we hear.

There are so many sources at work eroding our faith – Satan certainly has no interest in letting us believe and act on the authority given to us to make the kingdom more fully manifest in this world. Our own doubts also tear at our faith when we listen to symptoms or doctors' reports. Even well meaning loved ones erode our faith when they insist on hearing how bad the situation is, or when they share a story of another brother in the faith who succumbed to a situation "just like yours." Satan loves to goad people into explaining away God's promises in order to weaken our faith.

It is crucial to guard our mouths and our ears. There may actually be times when we have to remove ourselves from the repeated eroding effect of well intentioned people. You don't have to just sit and quietly listen to faith erosion. It is important to stay away from people who you know are going to persistently talk about the problem, or who seem to encourage you to talk against faith-building truth.

This can be a difficult area in which to gain victory, especially when we have been accustomed to not really guarding what words come out. Oh, sure, we civilized adults avoid crude language, nasty jokes, and vulgar swearing. But how often do we jokingly say belittling or degrading or sarcastic things about ourselves or our loved ones? It's just a joke, right?

Have you listened to how many times we say things like, "I'm so bad with names." "I've never been good with numbers." "I'm a horrible business person." "My kids always get the flu this time of year." "My wife is horrible with directions. She gets lost all the time." These flippant words give legal access to negative forces, empowering them to impact your life! How about, "My hypertension…", "My cancer…", "My arthritis…", "My allergies…", My bad genes…"? Do you really want to legally claim these health curses as your own? Stop saying it.

We have a choice – our words can be building blocks or wrecking balls. We can choose to speak edifying stability into our lives and the lives around us, or we can throw verbal stumbling blocks in our path. And, again, it is more than "just" words – God creates the fruit of the lips. (Isaiah 57:19)

Now this is not easy. We've spent years not being aware of the importance of this, and Satan loves it. He loves to hear us, all unaware, give him access to these areas of our lives. And he loves to hear us pooh-pooh the idea that our negative words matter at this level of spiritual encounter and warfare. It's almost as though our tongues have a mind of their own! (James 3:8 "But no one can tame the tongue; it is a restless evil and full of deadly poison.")

But it's time to change. So here is a challenge. (Colossians 4:6) **"Let your speech be always with grace, seasoned with salt, that ye may know how ye**

ought to answer every man." Every time you say a faith-eroding negative comment, stop yourself. Pray a prayer of repentance over what you just said, and replace that sentence with a promise from God's unalterable truth.

Did you hear yourself say, "My arthritis always acts up with cold weather"? Take a moment, ask God for forgiveness for that lie, and say something like, "I rebuke you, arthritis and inflammation in Jesus' name, and I command you to leave my body. And in that name, I command you, joints, to function perfectly. Lord, thank you for healthy joints." God's Word is clear in teaching us that words, both ours and God's, are important and powerful. **"…Man shall not live by bread alone, but by every word that proceedeth out of the mouth of God."** (Matthew 4:4)

God has given us authority to participate in creating a better future by believing His word and speaking it aloud. (Isaiah 57:19) **"I create the fruit of the lips… says the Lord…"** It has been said, "If we say what God said, then God will do what we say." A bold comment, yes? But think about it for a moment. God's word is Truth, and by agreeing with it, we are speaking with God. And because our spoken words are powerful, think of how much more powerful our spoken words are when they are in full agreement with His Word! Again, the spoken word gives legal permission for either God or Satan to work. Who would you prefer to have free access to your life? Let's get about the task of taming our mouth and training it to speak Truth, rather than opening a door wider for Satan to steal, kill and destroy us. Are you lacking something in your life that He promised? Find the supporting verses in His Word and speak them – audibly, frequently, and in faith. Believe them, claim them, speak them, and hold fast to them.

There is an important distinction to be understood here. I am not proposing the "name it and claim it" teachings of some disrepute. The only things we have a right to name and claim are the things that He has named, the things He has promised. It was God who told the weak to say "...**I *am* strong.**" (Joel 3:10) He commanded this because truth that God has ordained, spoken aloud with faith behind it, will change the material world to match the spiritual one. "**...and whatsoever thou shalt bind on earth** [with our spirit-led words] **shall be bound in heaven: and whatsoever thou shalt loose on earth shall be loosed in heaven.**" (**Matthew 16:19**)

So, while we cannot claim any old thing that we covet, we certainly do have a right to expect those things that He has told us are ours. He purchased them and offers them for our use in furthering His kingdom, so let us do our part in using His resources properly. Let us stop sabotaging His good work by speaking negatively about ourselves and our lives, and others and their lives.

One way to help us break this habit is to find a person of like belief, and ask them to help you catch the words. We often don't even hear ourselves doing it. But a good friend may hear it and ask if you really meant to say that.

Finally, it may help to understand that the Bible tells us to meditate on His Word, and to never stop speaking it. One definition and application of the word 'meditate' is "to mutter", or "to speak over and over." So find verses that apply to issues you are dealing with and meditate on them – speak them out loud over and over. This is how our faith is built into a force strong enough to change our situations. What we hear with our ears changes our faith power! Even when we are the ones speaking the truth. (Romans 10:17) **"So then faith cometh by hearing, and hearing by the word of God."** Likewise, listening to doubt-filled, or fear-filled words erodes our faith. Guard your ears as carefully as you guard your tongue.

An interesting alternate arrangement of this verse may read, "Faith comes from hearing and hearing the word of Christ." Hearing it over and over builds our faith, even as doubt and fear and the whispers of the enemy try to erode it.

If you examine the healings that Jesus did in the gospels, you will see a startling consistency in how often he is seen teaching the Word of God before healing anyone. I suspect this was because He needed to have people of strong faith to receive the truth of healing. So He gave them the word, and this increased their faith to the point where they were ready to receive the healing He offered. So, too, in our lives. We need to hear the word to increase the strength of our faith to the point where we can apply that truth, speak it boldly and receive those promises to change the circumstances of our lives.

Speak truth, consistently. Speak blessing and

edification over yourself, over your family members, and over your life. Take negative thoughts and negative words captive. Even King David knew he needed God's help with this. He prayed, **"Let the words of my mouth, and the meditation of my heart, be acceptable in thy sight, O LORD, my strength, and my redeemer."** (Psalm 19:14) Tame your tongue to avoid opening gates of ingress to the negative forces arrayed against us, for **"A man shall be satisfied with good by the fruit of *his* mouth..."** (Proverbs 12:14)

Chapter 14

Touching and Healing

O f all the topics in this book, none is more appropriate for Christian Chiropractors, and none is more controversial than miraculous signs of healing. Of all the healing arts, Chiropractic is the most 'hands-on'. Even with technology like Pro-Adjuster and other computer aided adjusting techniques, doctors touching patients with the intent of healing happens all day, every day in every Chiropractor's office.

So what do we do with this opportunity? How do we place in juxtaposition both the hands-on propensity of Chiropractic and the implicit command of Mark 16, verses 17 and 18? **"And these signs shall follow them that believe; In my name shall they cast out devils; they shall speak with new tongues; They shall take up serpents; and if they drink any deadly thing, it shall not hurt them; they shall lay hands on the sick, and they shall recover."**

Every day we come in contact with people who are either sick and in need of healing, lost and in need of Christ, or both. With this promise of Christ's, that we who believe will be accompanied with the sign of touching and healing, we are in a unique position both to heal those who are unwell, and to show God's love and power in this way.

I must confess that I am uneasy in writing this chapter,

because after 30 years of practice, and nine foreign mission trips, I have very few examples of touching and healing to show for it. Sure, there are instances where we got great results from adjusting people – a woman in Kenya who got instant relief after years of back pain with one adjustment, a child who walked after a series of three adjustments in Rochester, a man whose urine no longer had blood in it after one adjustment. But those can be explained away as wonderful examples of the power of Chiropractic as easily as by a touch of God.

My own journey into believing that we can touch and heal is relatively new. I've always known that God is a healing God, and that He can heal anything if He chooses to. But my new belief that we can carry this healing power to people now, that it certainly is His will that all be healed, just as it is His will that all be saved, that He has empowered us believers to touch and heal, is new to me.

Because of all of this, but especially because I am convinced of the truth of this issue, let me share with you an overview of the biblical support for my stance.

There are at least 30 different reasons to believe that it is God's will to heal every person. If you want more, I suggest that you obtain audio teaching by Pastor Keith Moore (www.moorelife.com) to learn in more detail. But for our purposes, let me list a few of the thirty.

- Just as it is God's will for every man to be saved (2 Peter 3:9) it is also His will for all who ask Him for it to be healed. (Luke 5) Now it is obvious that, even though it is His will for all to be saved, not everybody is saved. In the same way, though it is His will for all to be healed, not all are – for the same reasons. (See Chapter 17.)

- God's will ruled in Eden where there was no sickness before the fall. (Genesis 1:31) It is still His best will for all sickness to be gone.
- God's will is perfectly in place in heaven where, again, there is complete health for all, and we are told to pray for His will to be done here as it is in heaven. (Revelation 21:1-4, and Matthew 6:10)
- His word is medicine, and His word is for every person. (Proverbs 4:20)
- Sin is not His will, and sickness and death started with sin. (Romans 5:12)
- Sickness is a work of Satan, (Job 2:7) sickness is a curse, (Galatians 3, Deuteronomy 28) and sickness is oppression by the devil. (Acts 10:38)
- People glorify God when they are healed. (Luke 13:17) Granted, godly people do glorify God while they endure sickness, but I believe that is a second-runner-up to glorifying God for healing.
- One of God's eternal names is Jehova Rapha – The Lord your Healer. (Deuteronomy 7:9)
- He has already borne and carried our sicknesses. (Isaiah 53:4 and 1 Peter 2:24)
- My body is a member of Christ, and He would not want His body to be sick. (1 Corinthians 6:15)
- As a Father, He always gives good. (Matthew 7:7-11) He called healing "the children's bread."

(Matthew 15:28-28) Bread is a regular staple of good nutrition, not a rare treat for special occasions.

- The command to heal was given to the 12 apostles (Matthew 10:1), to the 72 (Luke 10:1-9), to church leaders (James 5:14-16), and to all believers! (Mark 16:15)
- He promises that, **"With long life I will satisfy you..."** (Psalm 91:16)

The biblical evidence goes on, but again, my experience is limited – for a number of reasons. I'd like to be able to say that it's mostly because I am only just beginning to learn of this authority. But I suspect that it's also a combination of my lack of boldness in taking a stance on this, and the smallness of my faith. (We'll discuss this more in Chapter 17.) But no more! From this day on, I am stepping out in building my faith and in acting on His promises.

A valid question is asked, "If it is God's will for all of His children to be healthy, why do we get sick at all?" I can think of two reasons, and there are probably more. One, we frequently walk outside of God's clear direction for how to be healthy. In diet, exercise, stress loads and other ways, we break the 'rules of the game' and pay a price.

Secondly, the Word tells us that there is a second player in the game. Satan is real, and he is looking for ways to "steal, kill, and destroy" us. So as he has opportunity, he throws punches at us. For instance, in the spring of 2009 I was involved in a significant car accident in which I broke my neck in three places, including a "burst" fracture of C-1. Humanly speaking, I should be dead or at least paralyzed. Satan intended to kill me, but God said, "This far, and no farther." My life was spared, I was healed and am back to full activities. This incident helped me realize the reality of Satan's desire to destroy us. As he has opportunity he will attack in many ways, with disease, with financial hardships, with relationship stresses, and more. But "greater is He who is in us, than he who is in the world." So we can shelter in God's protection, and when Satan attacks, we have the authority and the promises of Almighty God with which to fight back.

We can claim healing, provision, restoration and mercy in the face of any of the evil one's most vicious attacks – all because Jesus paid for them for us with His life, suffering, and death.

A bit more on this topic, just to whet your appetite? Of the 20 specific instances of Jesus healing people written of in the New Testament, there are some common denominators. Most of them clearly record the key ingredient of receiving healing to be the patient's faith. A few more of the instances merely insinuate that the patient's faith was a key component. Only three seem to be outside that pattern, and are considered examples of pure acts of mercy on the part of God.

It is interesting to note that almost every time Jesus healed, there came first a time of His teaching. What He taught on is usually not noted, but perhaps we can infer that since faith is necessary to receive healing, and faith is borne from hearing the Word of God, His teaching was designed to increase their faith to the point where they were in a place spiritually to receive the gift offered.

In several instances, Jesus had to remove the patient from the influence of unbelief (doubting family members or neighbors) in order to perform the healing. Again, the aim was to strengthen the faith of the one receiving the healing, and to minimize the factors that depleted the firmness of the faith through doubt or fear.

Yet another key principle in scriptural healing is the concept of jurisdictions, authority, and how our free will impacts the ability of a 'healer' to bring spiritual power to bear on a situation.

The concept of jurisdiction goes all the way back to God evicting Satan from heaven and consigning him to earth. In that historical event he gave the earth to Satan. Then, when man was created, God gave authority to man to subdue and steward the earth. Next, man, in his sin, gave that authority to Satan once again, and in fact Jesus described Satan as the prince of the world in John 12:31. In His death and resurrection Jesus finally took the keys of authority back from Satan, and in our new birth in Christ, we are given authority once again in this world.

All of that shows how jurisdiction is an important legal truth in spiritual matters. This concept plays out in our ministering to others. As creatures of free will, each person has the right to choose whether to submit to God's rule or Satan's. This choice continues throughout life, and is what gives legal permission for either God or

Satan to have access to our lives. This principle impacts everything that Christ purchased for us. While He died to save every person, only those who choose to submit to God's plan will avail themselves of it. While He purchased healing with His stripes, only those who believe this truth and submit to the simplicity of receiving it will be healed. Even though these things are available to all, He will never force them on anyone.

Practically speaking, this plays out in very matter-of-fact steps when we are attempting to minister healing to those who are oppressed with sickness. It is imperative to recognize that every person is a 'free agent' in their ability to believe, to have faith, and to receive what Christ offers.

Yet there are times when an individual is unable to understand, believe, or receive on their own. The most obvious situation is when a child is too young to understand or to make decisions on their own. In Mark 5 Jairus comes to Christ on behalf of his young daughter, and Jesus is able to respond and raise the child from the dead based on her father's faith. In Matthew 8 the centurion comes on behalf of his servant, and again, we see that Jesus is able to honor his faith and heal the servant. In these two examples, Jesus acknowledges that the men have jurisdictional authority to believe for another person.

In my own life, my wife interceded on my behalf when I was incapacitated in that car accident. She believed, and I was healed when I should have been dead. Then, as I regained my faculties, I was able to receive continued healing on my own, and the authority for receiving returned to my own jurisdiction. Together, we would often read aloud verses that promised healing. Over and over, we would proclaim the truth that I was healed – even when looking at x-rays that showed the fractures were not healing. Even when the surgeon recommended surgery to fuse C-4 and 5 because he felt the fractures were so instable. We spoke these verses and promises as truth, even when reports said otherwise. The Word is always more unchangingly true than mere reports.

As of this writing, my healing, purchased 2000 years ago at the whipping post, has manifest itself in my body to the point that I rarely even think about the injuries any more. C-4 and C-5, which were predicted to fuse as a natural consequence of the fractures through the facets, still move today – 2 years later. C-1, which could have shifted and killed me, and which should have produced arthritis and inflammation, is strong and healthy. He said that he took my sickness, and praise Him, He did! He said that I would leap like a calf from the stall, and praise His name, I can!

Yet another biblical example occurred when Jesus took a blind man outside the city limits in order to heal him. In Mark 8:12 Jesus had spoken a curse over the same area, telling them that no sign would be given to them, and giving the area over to Satan's jurisdiction. Also, after healing the demon possessed man in Matthew 8 the people had asked Jesus to leave the area, again leaving the area to the dominion of the evil one and the doubt that he loves. When he then encountered a man who had enough faith to be healed in verse 22, he had to honor that jurisdictional dominion and the lack of faith, and had to leave their influence in order to minister the healing. He then warned the man to stay away from the faith destroying influence of the people of that area – presumably to ensure that he keep his healing. All of this occurred within an area of about 7 miles in diameter.

So how does that impact our ability to minister healing to others? Each person must, of their own free will, allow God access to their heart in order to receive the grace He offers. This takes the form of honestly answering four questions that establish the strength of their faith, and give the minister (if a minister is involved in leading them through the process of understanding, believing and receiving) and then God himself, legal access to work with and in their spirit, leading to manifestation of grace in the physical realm. At each of these questions, permission is either granted or denied to move ahead through the process of ministering and receiving healing.

Question 1: May I pray for you? May I speak freely to you about this matter?

- This question gives permission to the minister to help the seeker find truth. It is an important step in granting jurisdictional authority in ministry.

Question 2: Do you believe that God can heal you? Does He have the ability to change your physical situation in such a way that you are healed?

- This question lays the foundation of God's

power and reality. It is a way of asking if the seeker accepts the Word of God as ultimate truth. If this question is answered with a 'yes' then the next question can be addressed, and built upon to strengthen faith for receiving healing and other gifts offered by Him.

Question 3: Does He want to heal you? Is it His will right now to heal you?

-    This is a key question in accessing the power of God. If there is any wavering on this it reveals a lack of faith – a lack of ability to take hold of the gift of healing that was purchased with Christ's stripes. As long as question #2 is answered positively, the seeker can grow into the right frame of mind for question #3 because the Word of God teaches clearly that healing is indeed God's will for every believer.

Question 4: Do you want Him to heal you? Is there any reason why you want to hang on to your oppression?

-    What a strange question! Yet it is interesting to see how many reasons people may have for hanging on to their illness. Some find their illness to be a critical part of their identity – they only know how to interact with others through the habits learned by being sick. Others have financial support based on having a diagnosed illness. Some get sympathy over being sick. Still others use their illness as an excuse to avoid activities or events. They either love their disease, or find it frightening to face life without it. People must confront this issue in order to take hold of the healing that is already theirs.

Each of these questions must be answered honestly and in the affirmative in order for God's healing power to be manifest. It is already paid for and available, but any time a person answers "no" to one of these questions, they are barring God from acting on their behalf, and allowing sickness and brokenness to rule in their life. If the answer is no, the minister must honor their denial of healing, and either gently attempt to teach them the truth, or back away from the encounter. God is legally barred from acting, and the minister will only cause more resistance by proceeding to attempt to minister healing. The healing will likely fail, and the person's accumulated experiences denying healing will be strengthened, giving them yet another reason to doubt God's ability or willingness to heal.

In each case, the seeker must gain knowledge of God's plan and purpose, and faith in the teaching to receive what God is offering. Recall that faith comes from hearing and hearing (again) the Word of God. So dealing with these questions must come from the Word, and not mere logic, man's reasoning, or argument. These are spiritual matters, and it is the spirit that must embrace these truths, not merely the mind.

A negative answer to Question #1 reveals a heart that does not want to deal with you as a minister of healing, or that rejects the Bible as the source of truth. Dealing with this requires discernment of which of these is the hindrance and a gentle introduction of the claims of the Bible.

If Questions #2 is answered in the negative, pray for discernment and lead the seeker through verses that show God's ability to heal.

Old Testament examples include:
- The leprous court official, Naaman – 2 Kings 5
- Miriam's experience with leprosy – Numbers 12
- Hezekiah the king – 2 Kings 20
- The widow's son – 1 Kings 17

New Testament examples abound, and include:
- The boy raised from the dead – Luke 7
- The centurion's servant – Matthew 8
- Jairus's daughter – Mark 5
- The blind man – Mark 8
- The man living among the tombs – Mark 5
- All who were ill – Matthew 4

If the seeker acknowledges that the Bible is true, then at some point these stories will convey the point that God can, indeed, heal anyone of any disease.

Question #3 uncovers an important point of faith. In most churches Christians agree that God, being God, can do anything and heal anything. Anything! But for various reasons they tend to make excuses for why healing may happen at times, but that God may want to leave a person in their sickness and oppression to achieve a different good, or to teach a life lesson, or to strengthen character. This must be dealt with in each individual in order to minister or receive healing. The list of 13 reasons a few pages back can serve as a scripture list to build knowledge and faith on this topic. Remember, not one single person who came to Jesus for healing was turned away without it.

Question #4 deals with subtle issues of the heart. Sometimes simply discussing the question will reveal an attitude that the seeker was not even aware of, and once it is exposed can be repented of and corrected. It may also reveal a spiritual stronghold over which Satan has control (improper dependence or addiction to medication or attention, etc.), and it must be rebuked and taken back before healing can be accomplished.

Jesus asked some form of each of these questions in one or more of the examples of healing that He ministered in the gospels. Of the blind man in Luke 18 He asked, "What do you want me to do for you?" Seeing that he was convinced that He could heal, He assured the leper in Luke 5 that He was also willing to heal. In John chapter 5, Jesus asked the man by the Pool of Bethesda if he wanted to get well.

In some cases the Holy Spirit revealed to Jesus that the person's answer was 'Yes! Yes! And Yes!" to all three questions, so their faith was already at the point to receive healing. In the example of the paralytic brought by his four friends and let down through a hole in the roof, it was obvious that they believed that He could (else they would not have come to the meeting), and that He would (else they would not have forced their way into His presence), and that the man desired release from his malady (or he would not have tolerated being hauled about the town), so Jesus went ahead and ministered healing to him. But unless the Spirit reveals similar answers before the questions are asked, it will be appropriate for us to actually ask the questions.

If He found the answers to these questions important enough to ask for them and to note in the gospels, we should pay attention, and follow His example.

As for the hierarchy of jurisdictions, parents have the authority to answer for their children in spiritual matters up until the child understands the meaning of these concepts. In similar fashion, a spouse has authority to answer for their incapacitated 'other half', a boss has limited authority in some areas of life for an employee, a pastor for parishioners, and so on. The jurisdictions among various relationships go back to hierarchies established by God in the Old Testament. In answering the four questions, jurisdictional authority is honored.

There are times, too, when authority may be temporarily bestowed upon a person who desires to minister on behalf of others. If a parent does not feel qualified to minister healing to a child, they may verbally authorize another to minister in their place. These are spiritual legalities that must be observed in order for us to be effective in ministering healing in our sphere of influence.

So what of us in our circle of influence? I can only offer you what I am intending to move toward in my life. I intend to continue digging into His word, both for knowledge on how healing is accomplished, and to build my own faith in ministering and receiving healing.

I intend to move more and more in the direction of boldness in going beyond the already powerful healing offered in Chiropractic, and to offer healing in the name of Jesus Christ.

Let's summarize some key principles that are indicated in scripture to make offering healing effective:

- Lines of authority and jurisdiction must be honored. Ask the four questions.
- If the questions reveal a lack of either knowledge or faith, STOP. Deal with the hindrances to healing before going on.
- Offer healing in the name of Jesus Christ. This is important, so that no confusion rises as to the source of the healing.
- Offer healing in faith, knowing that what God has promised, He will perform.
- Offer healing audibly. Again, the spoken word is powerful in spiritual matters.
- Offer healing at the leading of the Holy Spirit. Only by their answers to the four questions, and by this leading, can we know the state of the patient's faith. How else can we know that their faith is strong enough to receive the healing that is offered?
- Offer follow-up for the patient's continued growth and health. Satan hates to lose battles and will seek to take back what was lost in the healing. He will not give up seeking to steal their health back, to destroy their health, or to outright kill.
- With spiritual discernment, teach patients not only Chiropractic, but the things of faith. For with hearing the Word of God, faith is built – both for salvation and for healing.

Touching and healing. I am excited to more boldly step out into this arena of my professional life. Where will it lead? I trust and expect to see greater fruit, a stronger witness, and a larger investment in the kingdom of God.

Chapter 15

Effective Prayer

What we refer to as prayer may be both simpler and more 'partitioned' than we first think. Literally, prayer means talking with God. A pretty simple concept, and God loves for us to do it. He wants us to fellowship with Him, and to spend time in His presence– pouring our heart out to Him, and taking time to listen. That's why Jesus died, after all, to purchase a way for us to return to that fellowship.

We could also look at prayer, however, as three distinct types of interactions with Him.

1. When faced with an attack by Satan, an attempt by him to kill, steal or destroy our lives, we are given authority to 'speak to the mountain'. We are to speak directly to the problem and command it, with the authority given to us by Jesus, to get out of our lives. This would include common life challenges such as:

   a. Sickness – Just as Jesus spoke to Peter's mother-in-law's fever. We are authorized to command sickness to leave.

   b. Poverty – Jesus became poor so that we might become rich. When we have missed God's leading in areas that have led to slavery to debt, we can repent of those mistakes, and then command debt to leave.

c. Demonic influence, attack or stronghold – Just as Jesus cast out 'Legion' from the man near the tombs, we have been given authority over every spiritual attack or stronghold.

2. Another way to look at these modes of battle against Satan's plans for us involve the words 'bind' and 'resist'. We are authorized and ordered to use these modes of power encounters against the various attacks of the evil one. Use verbal commands in the name of the Lord Jesus Christ to resist and bind Satan's plans, his power, his intentions, his attacks. These are examples of speaking to the problem with authority to use the power given to us by God. It's His power. He has given us authority to use it.

3. When we find ourselves in need of something that Jesus purchased for us during His time here on earth, we are authorized to come and receive it. Claiming a promise offered to us is not presumptuous. Rather, it is expected as loved children coming to a good father who longs to give good things. We can, with full assurance and boldness, learn of the promises made by Him, and claim them for ourselves in areas such as:

a. Salvation – whosoever will may come.

b. Health – by His stripes we are healed, and all who touched Him were healed.

c. Prosperity – He became poor so that we might become rich.

d.   Protection – a thousand may fall at my side… but it will not come near me.

      e. Leading – He makes the crooked path straight.

      f. Wisdom – He gives to all liberally, when we ask without wavering.

4. These are times when, once we know what has been purchased by Christ for us, (See Substitutions and Examples in Chapter 17) and once we believe in our heart what He said, we can boldly receive them, or grab hold of them by faith. We no longer need to beg Him for these things, but may receive them by faith. And when Satan comes again to try to convince us otherwise, we must speak the word aloud, and cling all the tighter to what is ours. This is believing and receiving.

5. And then there are times when we just need to be in His presence and share our hearts with Him. This is a combination of seeking His face, basking in His Word, and listening for the still small voice as He gives light to our path. This is where true worshippers come in spirit and in truth to simple bow and honor Him in private. These are times of resting, of growing our faith by meditating on, or speaking His word aloud to ourselves. This is where we get to share our dreams and desires with Him, and then trust Him to, "... do exceeding abundantly above all that we ask or think, according to the power that works in us," (Ephesians 3:20)

6. So prayer is not begging God for things. It is not asking Him over and over in an effort to wear Him down. It is not an attempt to pry

good things out of the stingy hand of Almighty
God. It is not proving how deserving we are by
persisting in prayer.

7. Prayer is either receiving through faith what He
    has already offered, or using the authority given to
    us by Christ, or quietly sharing with and listening
    to our loving Father. Speaking to the problems we
    face, believing and receiving what He has already
    purchased for us, or quietly sharing our heart of
    hearts with Him.

8. Of course, faith is a key component of all three of
    these portions of prayer. Faith, again, is acting on a
    truth that has been given by a credible source, even
    if we cannot see, feel or measure that truth at the
    time. Faith is believing that His promises, given in
    His Word, are more real than what our eyes see.

9. The spoken Word is a second key component
    to effective, powerful prayer, since it is with the
    heart that we believe, yet with the mouth that
    we confess truth and receive it. So speak up –
    audibly – in order to enjoy spiritual impact in this
    physical world.

10. Again, here in the matter of effective prayer, just
    as in so many other areas of our spiritual life, the
    spoken word is critical. Don't hesitate to speak
    aloud in all three areas of prayer, even if you are
    by yourself. Confession is "agreeing with what
    He says about any given topic." When we speak
    aloud the Truth that we find in His written Word,
    things around us change. This is powerful and
    effective prayer.

Chapter 16

Sowing and Reaping

I t seems to be a pretty consistent pattern in the Word
that God teaches principles in this way:

- The truth is taught in the written Word
- That truth is then demonstrated in an analogy
  seen in the physical world
- When we believe that truth deep in our heart –
  not simply in our mind – it comes out in our
  spoken words
- Our spoken word, in agreement with the written
  Word, empowered by our faith that it will
  happen as we speak, changes our physical world

As we live our lives here on this planet, stewarding
the gift of our lives, the Master expects us to sow
significant seed, in order to reap eternal harvest. This is
perhaps at least a partial definition of spiritual maturity,
spiritual growth, and lasting purpose.

In fact, seeing how much He has invested in us, from
our very existence to His redeeming us from our sins,
and His continued work in us to bring us to maturity
and Christ-likeness, it is understandable that He expects
some fruit from His investment.

This topic of seed, harvest and fruitfulness actually
has three areas of application:

-   My own soul and spirit can receive the seed of

the Word, and this is supported in the parable of the sown seed, as well as in the verse where John prays that we prosper in all things even as our soul prospers. (3 John 1:2)

-   In the same way, we can sow seed in others' hearts. Their 'soil' can either yield a harvest in their own lives, or they can refuse to receive it and fail to bring forth any fruit.

-   Likewise, we can sow into ministries with our finances, time and talents, and expect a harvest from it.

In each of these three areas of sowing, we can expect to reap a harvest as long as certain conditions are met. For maturation does not just happen. Growth, maturity and fruit bearing require care and nurture, particularly if we desire fruit that will last. In the 15th chapter of John, Jesus discusses how seriously God takes our fruitfulness. A study of that passage, as well as the 4th chapter of Mark, reveal a ton of insight into sowing, fruitfulness, harvesting and God's husbandry of our heart.

Here are some thoughts to 'prime the pump' on the rich topic of fruitfulness:

-   We are responsible to plant good seed – choose carefully what seed you allow into the 'soil' of your own heart, and what seed you plant in the hearts of those around you. Speak truth! All seed will produce growth similar to whence it came. Truth from the Word of God will produce fruit of lasting, righteous value in our own hearts, in the hearts of other hearers, and in the ministries into which we sow. Likewise, fleshly seed will produce fruit of doubt and death if we let it grow.

- In our own heart, we can decide if we are providing good soil – a heart that is willing to receive, be invaded by, and respond to growing seed. When we are sowing in others hearts, we can pray for and discern if there is good soil or rocky soil. There are times when we should hold onto our seed until good soil is located. "Don't cast your pearls before swine." This requires the leading of the Holy Spirit. Knowing where to sow our resources is entirely a matter of spiritual insight.

- Keep in mind the fact that sowing is an analogy that has several applications.
  o We sow seed of the Word in our own heart by hearing the Word of God.
  o We sow seed in the hearts of others by sharing Truth with them.
  o We sow seeds of time, skills, finances and other resources by giving to Kingdom related ministries and ministers.

- Seed requires water in order to grow – Truth and seed are both breathed upon and made alive by the Holy Spirit.

- Fertilizer adds nutrients essential for growth and fruitfulness – Our faith to believe, receive and act upon His promises and truth acts to nourish the growing seeds.

- Sun – As we spend time in His presence, meditating on and listening to His word and voice, our hearts are warmed, providing another ingredient to healthy harvest.

- Weeding – With godly discernment, God will

prune away unproductive growth. This includes, lies, sin, fear, and other negative portions of our lives that are strangling our testimony and effectiveness.

• Pruning – And when we are being productive for His cause, He then prunes us, cutting off growth that is not as productive as they could be – even 'good' things can hinder the better things.

• Harvest – It is good to expect and prepare for a harvest of fruit. When we sow evangelism, we should expect souls to be won. When we sow encouragement and edification, we should expect people to grow in their faith and walk. When we sow time into volunteering for the Kingdom, it is good to expect our time to be multiplied. When we sow financially, we can boldly expect to harvest greater financial blessing. Since we have been faithful with a little, we will be entrusted with more. At the same time, if we expect nothing back from our efforts, the harvest will likely sit in the field unharvested, doing no one any good. Expect!

One of the most important goals for a Christian is to bear eternal fruit. There are hundreds of ways in which to do this. As we hear and obey His leading to sow good seed in good soil, our lives will produce many times the quantity we sow in faith.

Chapter 17

Conclusion: What if it ain't workin'?

As I consider the ministry power and authority that have been entrusted to us, I find myself wondering how I can be more effective in defeating Satan's plans, and more accomplished in using the weapons handed to me. I wonder why more people are not healed at my touch. Why are so few of my prayers answered in miraculous ways? Why does my life not look more like the life of Jesus, or Paul, or John?

The life of Christ, as tracked in the gospels, is so full and deep that a hundred books, written over a hundred lifetimes, could never reach the depths of what He offered, taught, and accomplished in his three years of ministry. It is interesting to consider the fact that what we read in the written accounts of His life is just a sampling of all the things He did. (John 21:25) **"And there are also many other things which Jesus did, the which, if they should be written every one, I suppose that even the world itself could not contain the books that should be written. Amen."** What we see in the gospels is just a sampling! But a specific sampling – a special and deliberate selection of the things He did.

So how did God choose these events out of all the many actions done, words spoken, and miracles performed? Why did He choose these items to hand down to us, and leave out so many others? Surely not just by chance. The stories and events portrayed in the gospels are certainly not just the ones that the apostles happened to recall as they wrote the accounts. I suspect that Almighty God picked the events that He chose for a reason – that those events were included to teach us specific things about what Jesus did, and specific things that He wanted to hand down to us.

Since it is true that Jesus told us that **"… greater works than these shall he do"**, and it is true that we are to aim to be like Him, I suggest that we are to learn how to do things like pray, heal, and sow fruitful seed from the way He did these things.

As you consider just how impactful a life lived with this power and authority will be, remember (John 14:12) **"Verily, verily, I say unto you, He that believeth on me, the works that I do shall he do also; and greater *works* than these shall he do; because I go unto my Father."**

So is this miracle-working life meant for us today, or just for the 12 apostles? Matthew 10:1-8, and Luke 9:1 tell the story of Jesus sending the 12 out endued with this authority. And Luke 10:8-9 shows that it was intended for 72 more. Then we see in James 5:15 that elders in the church, years after Jesus ascended back into heaven, were authorized to function in this way. And I fully believe that the message of Mark 16:17-18 teaches the truth that He intends all believers to be just as authorized to function with miraculous proofs of His power.

I have found that one way to look at the Lessons of

Christ's Life, a way to examine His life that might make it a bit easier to follow in His footsteps, is to divide His actions into two categories: Substitutions and Examples.

Substitutions are things that He did for us – in our place. They are things that He did as a onetime only event that made it so that we would not ever have to do those things for ourselves. These are the things that most of us are taught in the early years of our search for, and walk with, Christ. Here is a short list – probably incomplete, but it certainly shows what we have to be thankful for.

Substitutions:

- I should have died, but He did instead – giving me life – Romans 6:23
- I should have been judged guilty, but He was instead – taking my punishment – Isaiah 53:4-6
- I should have bled, but He did instead – taking my sins away – Psalm 103:12
- I should have taken the stripes, but He did instead – taking my sickness – Isaiah 53:5 and 1 Peter 2:24
- I earned God's wrath, but He satisfied it – taking my rejection – 1 Thessalonians 1:10
- He became poor so that I might become rich – taking my poverty – 2 Corinthians 8:9

What can we say other than "Thank you!" from a position of humble gratitude, as we contemplate what He did for us as the ultimate Substitute.

Examples, on the other hand, are things that He did to show us how to do life and ministry. They are the items to which He was referring when He said, "Greater things than these you will do." How exciting is that? When you think about the amazing things that Jesus did as He walked this planet in the form of a man, having set aside His Godlike powers, (Philippians 2:6-7) **"Who, being in the form of God, thought it not robbery to be equal with God: But made himself of no reputation, and took upon him the form of a servant, and was made in the likeness of men."**, consider how they apply to us doing 'greater things'!

It is true. He did set aside His God-powers when he came to earth. He did no miracles during his first 30 years on earth. Not one! (John 2:11) He did nothing of the sort until after He was baptized by the Holy Spirit – the same Holy Spirit that seals us at the moment of our salvation.

So how, you wonder, did He know what He knew? How did He heal as He did? How did He command nature and cast out demons as He did? By the leading and power of the same Holy Spirit that indwells us!

Here is a partial list of the things He did as examples during His time here on earth:

- He did only what the Father had Him do – John 8:28
- He listened to and obeyed the Holy Spirit – John 14:26 (exemplified 93 times in the New Testament)
- He was light and has left us to be the light – John 8:12, 9:5, Matt. 5:14
- He shared truth (78 times in the New Testament

He says something pertaining to "I tell you the truth") – John 16:7
- He touched and healed and gave – Mark 16:17-18
- He was perfect – we are called to be, also – Matt. 5:48
- He took authority over nature – we can, too, as we are led by the Holy Spirit – Matthew 8:23-25
- He was persecuted – we will be too – Mark 10:30

Still, with all of this said, I have lived years on end without seeing much done by God, through me, in anything like a miraculous way. How can this be? If it's His will for us to be healed, if it's His authority we carry about to do wonders proving His hand on our lives, if it's already been purchased for us – why don't we see the impact in practical ways around us?

There are several possible reasons:

- Sin in our lives will interfere with our communion and walk with God. The young nation of Israel "grieved and limited the Holy One" by complaining and rebelling against His ways. (Psalm 78:40-41)

- Lack of faith is a strong deterrent to our ability to receive the promised power, authority and blessings that He purchased for us. Just as people miss out on salvation because they don't believe, we may miss out on blessings and power-filled ministry due to a lack of faith. Just because we have faith to receive His gift of salvation, does not necessarily mean we will have faith to be healed, to walk in power, or to be blessed in other ways.

- Lack of knowledge of what He offers will stop our efforts cold. How can we believe the gifts are ours when we don't know what they are? This is part of why biblical teaching is so important. We must learn what He has done in order to have faith in His desire for us to have it.

So what are the solutions for a life devoid of the signs and wonders promised in the Bible? They are things we've all heard of our whole Christian lives. But now, knowing a bit more of what's at stake, perhaps we'll be more diligent in consistently pursuing them.

- Walk holy – don't make excuses to sin. "It is finished" means something!
- We are delivered and free from slavery to sin. Let's live like it.
- We are already crucified – and the life we live is lived by faith in Christ living in us.
- He is so willing to lead us, and His way is so much better, let us listen and obey.
- Learn what He purchased for us
- Get in the word – that is how we find out the truth.
- Learn words of faith, rather than words that explain away these power portions of the gospel.
- Grow your faith
- Hear the Word of God frequently – that is how faith is grown and strengthened.
- Listen and obey – those who were either saved or healed in the New Testament were able to

believe and receive their salvation and healing AFTER HEARING. Our faith, too, comes by hearing His words of truth.

Many reject these tenets of power and authority because it is seen so rarely in our churches. Caution! Never fall into the trap of explaining away His words to match our experience, or our lack of experience, or the stories of other Christians – no matter how great of a saint they may be. Rather, believe what He said, and find out why your experience is not measuring up to what He offered and paid for.

Even if, in a worst case scenario, you go years without seeing a person healed, a soul saved, a storm calmed, a mountain cast into the sea, a prayer miraculously answered – even if you struggle for your entire career to pay bills, and never leave a financial heritage for your descendants – so what?

Would you not rather, as I would, enter through the gates of pearl, have Jesus lift your chin to look you in the eye and hear Him say, "Well done, child! You believed what I said. You did your best to act in faith. You traded your minutes wisely in seeking me. You invested your life in eternal things as I told you to in my Word. Well done." Then I expect He will put His arm around my shoulders, lead me to my new home, and gently explain where I got it right and where I missed it.

Far better that, than to doubt and explain away His words to fit our wretched excuse of a spiritually dry existence, lived ineffectually because we didn't dig in and build our faith.

Consider this story.

A man grew up in the hills of Tennessee. Life was hard there, and he struggled to enjoy his life. But one day, he heard about a beautiful place called California where the weather was perfect, jobs were plentiful, and people had it easy. He realized, as he aged, that his life in Tennessee offered him nothing, so he decided to make the trip to California from Tennessee. A caring uncle heard of his decision and offered him a brand new Bentley Azure T, a three hundred thousand dollar car, for the trip. The man gratefully accepted the offer, since he was going to have to walk the entire distance otherwise – he had no resources for the trip other than a desire to get to this wonderful land he had heard so much about.

His uncle handed him the keys and began to explain the wonders of this amazing automobile to him, and to tell him about the debit card he had stashed in the glove box to pay for his gas and food on the trip. But the man was so excited to hit the road that he took the keys for the car and headed west. As he drove off, the uncle tried to stop him, but was only able to shout at the diminishing figure, "At least read the owner's manual!"

The excited traveler waved in the mirror, but failed to catch his uncle's parting words.

As he drove, he encountered many adventures, including snow covered roads, flat tires, baking heat, weary hours behind the wheel, and a blown gasket when he forgot to fill the oil reservoir. Along the way, he never opened the windows, or turned on the heat or air conditioning. Through all of this he persevered, and the trip took seven years because he had to stop along the way to work odd jobs to pay for gas, for tire repairs, for an engine overhaul, and because he repeatedly got lost along the way.

At no point did he ever doubt that he was going to arrive in California, and indeed, he did finally make it – weary, worn out, and with a good bit of doubt that it was really worth it since the trip was so difficult.

As he settled into his new home, one of his new friends listened to the story of his trip with incredulity. Finally, he said to him, "I'm so glad you made it! But do you realize that your trip could have been so much easier if you had paid attention to the owner's manual? It would have told you about the climate control, the GPS to guide your way, and the repair services that come free of charge with this great automobile." And when he opened the glove box to get the manual out, he noticed the debit card placed there by his uncle.

Of course this analogy is imprecise, but it is much like us and our trip through this life to heaven. The final destination is assured as long as we have chosen to follow Christ. We know where we are going. But the trip can be much easier, more interesting, and more fruitful if we use the "options" that come with the relationship.

This life is lived in the middle of a broken world. But our journey is led and empowered by our Master. He leads and authorizes us to use His gifts as signs of our heavenly citizenship, and to impact others along the way. We are to steward those resources in such a way as to see His kingdom come on this earth even as it is in heaven. And then someday we will arrive at the gates and finally see our King. And it will be good.

Let me close with a quote from Steven Furtick:

"By God's grace, no matter what it costs me, I'm going to live by audacious faith. I'm going to believe God for the impossible, to accomplish by and for him what I cannot accomplish on my own. No matter what people think about my vision for my life, I'm going to take God at his word..."

Knowing Him, believing Him, and acting on His promises is what makes it possible to live above the level of the tree tops. Living this way, both in your practice and in the rest of your life, is what makes it possible to leave a heritage that will last throughout eternity.

APPENDIX A

- **Question Number 1**: What will motivate my life – self, or Christ?
- **Question Number 2**: What sets you, as a Christian Chiropractor, apart and above any other ethical Chiropractor?
- **Question Number 3**: What does your office say, shout, or whisper to the people who enter?
- **Question Number 4**: Is it ever ethical to cheat, cut corners or lie?
- **Question Number 5**: Why did you hire the staff you hired? What do you expect out of your staff?
- **Question Number 6**: At what point do we shift from 'being light' to sharing the word?
- **Question Number 7**: How do we maximize our income generating potential while also staying true to our call to meeting needs and pointing people toward God?'
- **Question Number 8**: What are you willing to trade for a new patient?
- **Question Number 9**: Who needs your care anyway?
- **Question Number 10**: Is it ethical to sell 'stuff' to patients?
- **Question Number 11**: How well do you know the condition of your business?
- **Question Number 12**: How are wishes like fishes?

APPENDIX B

3 Patient Information Letters on

Spiritual Interest

(See Chapter 5 – Sharing the Gospel)
High Interest Level

On your initial paperwork in our office you indicated that you have high interest in spiritual matters. This indicates to me that you are well along on your spiritual journey. It is always exciting to me to see people who are moving along on their spiritual quest in life. Of course it is not a simple matter to find that way, because there are many 'religions' available to the person who seeks spiritual guidance. So please allow me to share my experience with you.

Of the many religions there are in our world, only one teaches that there is absolutely nothing that we can do to earn God's pleasure. The Bible teaches that we are separated from Him by our sin, and that we cannot make up for that by doing good. It teaches that being good may be good, but it's not good enough to clean the sin out of our past. There's simply no way to balance the good vs. bad in our lives by doing more good. The stain left by sin is permanent.

Fortunately for us, God loves us so much that He made the ultimate sacrifice in order to give us a way back to Him. While the penalty for our sin is death, He paid that penalty with His Son's own life. So if we are willing to admit our sin, and ask forgiveness, He is willing to mark the penalty as "Paid In Full", and give us a clean slate, a new heart, and eternity to walk and live with Him. All it takes is our admission of guilt, our decision to sin no more, and our trust in His Son as having paid our penalty.

Once that is done, the journey really only just begins. At that point we must begin to learn how to live in light of our new relationship with our Creator, Savior and Lord. And that is the catch. Living with Him as Lord rather than with our own desires as lord, is a challenging way of life, and one that can only be done by implementing four things consistently in our lives.

1) Reading the Bible every day
2) Spending time in prayer
3) Finding friends who will encourage us in this walk
4) Obeying whatever He asks us to do

Let me encourage you, wherever you are in your spiritual journey, to press on to the next step. If you have not accepted Jesus as your Savior and Lord, do so today. If you have, but are not regularly doing the above four steps, choose one and work on it each day. If you are doing those, then raise the standard a notch, and move closer yet to Him.

There are many distractions and counterfeits that can turn us from our relationship with God. Therefore, continue to check your path against the map – the Word of God. This is indeed an adventure. Let's put all that we can into it, for the rewards are tremendous and eternal when we invest our lives in the things of God.

Medium Interest Level

In your initial paperwork in our office you indicated that you have a moderate level of interest in spiritual matters. It is always exciting to me to see people who are moving along on their spiritual journey. The matters of eternity, life, death, and spiritual health are critical to us being truly healthy, and in fact are of more importance than simple physical health.

I say this because, while it is important to be physically healthy, still, no matter how healthy a person is, and no matter how thoroughly they seek physical health, every person still eventually dies. At that time, it matters little how health they were. All that matters is what preparation they made for the next phase of their life – eternity.

In light of this, let me encourage you to consider the claims of the Bible. There are many religions available to the person who seeks spiritual guidance. However, I have found that they all really break down into two basic categories.

- Those which seek to tell us how we can please God
- Those which seek to tell us how God is reaching out to us

I have found that almost all religions fit in the first category. The result of this is a lot of methods – many contradictory to each other – that try to teach us how to act better and thus earn God's approval.

Only the Bible teaches the second category. In fact the Bible makes it clear that there is absolutely nothing that we can do to please God. It teaches that being good may be good, but it's not good enough to clean the slate of our past. But it also makes it clear that He loves us so much that 2000 years ago He made a new way available for the asking. Here are the three basic claims of the Bible.

1) The Bible is true. My research tells me that it is true, and that it makes it clear that God is real, and that He made you, and loves you. In fact the book of John says, "God loved people so much that He gave His own Son, Jesus, so that anyone who believes in Him would be saved."

2) The fact that God cares about my life requires a response from me. The Bible teaches that because God is real and perfect, His desire to draw us into His family is restricted by sin in our lives. The process of being reconciled to God involves us recognizing our sin, asking for Him to forgive us for it, and accepting His free gift of forgiveness and eternal life. Romans says, "All have sinned, but the free gift of God is eternal life."

3) Accepting His gift of forgiveness does not necessarily make for an easier life. But it does guarantee that as we walk through this life with Him, our life has purpose and value that will last for eternity. Again, the book of John says, "If we trust Him we are no longer under judgment, but have forgiveness, and pass from death into life." It

goes on, "He created you and me for good works – even from the start of eternity."

If this makes sense to you, please consider making the Bible a part of your regular – even daily – reading. Most importantly, take the step of asking God for forgiveness so that you can start your new life as His own child. Then tell someone. It would be great news for me to hear that you have made God your Savior and Lord!

Low to No Interest Level

In your initial paperwork here at our office, you indicated either a low or no interest in spiritual matters. In light of the importance of this matter we felt that we should encourage you to consider the claims of the Bible. The claims of this ancient, yet completely up-to-date book, are supported by science, archeology, history and personal experience. It makes some fascinating claims about you and your destiny, and if it is true, as I am convinced that it is, then it begs some sort of response to those claims.

Ignoring this subject, and the Bible, will result in consequences that will affect you both now, during your life, as well as throughout eternity.

I would ask that you consider the following three things.

1. Why am I here? I believe that there is great hope and strength in knowing that God made us and has a plan for each one of us to live a significant life. If we are here for no reason other than to live,

work and die, then it just isn't worth it. Consider the concepts of good and bad, the existence of matters outside our understanding. There seems to be much to indicate the existence of life after death.

2. Is the Bible true? As I indicated above, I think that the Bible is authenticated by research of many kinds. It ends up that believing that there is no God is much like believing that a fully functioning 747 Jumbo Jet could be fashioned by a tornado striking a junk yard. It actually takes a greater leap of faith to believe that we are here by chance than to look at the evidence and conclude that God exists and He wants us to know Him.

3. Can we really know God? The Bible says that we can not only know Him, but we can know that He loves us, takes care of us, and wants us to live our lives in daily communication with Him. In fact it tells us that we can have a relationship with the Creator of the universe simply by acknowledging our mistakes, accepting His gift of forgiveness and His payment for the penalty of our sins, and agreeing to do what He asks us to do in the Bible.

If you want to know more about any of this, please do two things. First, be honest with God. Tell Him that you are no convinced, but that you would like to know more about Him. If you are sincere, He will begin to show Himself to you in small, yet important ways.

Second, feel free to ask us for more information. We have resources available, as well as time to talk with you about any of this. We want your health to be complete, not just physical. We want to encourage you to make your health well rounded, and a step along your own spiritual journey is an important part of the complete picture. Most of all, we want you to be prepared to deal with the reality that eternity waits, and your condition in eternity depends upon how you prepare for it now.

APPENDIX C

Verses on Healing

(Most of these verses I have placed here in a personalized format to give you an idea of how we can make them our own. They are also listed in a daily dose that I use in my own quiet times.)

- MONDAY:
    - He is the God that heals me. Ex. 15:26
    - The plague shall not be unto me because of the blood. Ex. 12:13
    - He will take all sickness away from me. Deut. 7:15
    - He turned the curse into a blessing because He loved me. Deut. 23:5 and Neh. 13:2
    - He has redeemed me from every sickness and every plague. Deut. 28:61 and Gal. 3:13
    - As my days, so shall my strength be. Deut. 33:25
    - He has healed me and kept me from going down to the pit. Ps. 30:1, 2

- TUESDAY:
    - He will give me strength, and bless me with peace. Ps. 29:11
    - He will preserve me and keep me alive. Ps. 41:2

- He will strengthen me on the bed of languishing. Ps. 41:3
- He is the health of my countenance and my God. Ps. 43:5
- No plague shall come near my dwelling. Ps. 91: 10
- He heals all my diseases. Ps. 103:3
- He sent His word and healed me, and delivered me from my destructions. Ps. 107:20
- Trusting Him brings health to my belly, and marrow to my bones. Pr. 3:8

- WEDNESDAY:
  - His words are life to me, and health/medicine to all my flesh. Pr. 4:22
  - A merry heart does good like a medicine. Neh. 8:10, Pr. 17:22
  - The lame man shall leap as a hart. Isa. 35:6
  - He will recover me, and make me to live. He is ready to save me. Isa. 38:16, 20
  - He will renew my strength. He will strengthen and help me. Isa. 40:31, 41:10
  - With His stripes I am healed. Isa. 53:5
  - He will heal me. Isa. 57: 19
  - My light shall break forth as the morning and my health shall spring forth speedily. Isa. 58:8
  - He will restore health unto me, and He will heal me of my wounds. Jer. 30:17

- THURSDAY:
  - He will bring health and cure, and He will cure me, and will reveal unto me the abundance of peace and truth. Jer. 33:6
  - He will bind up that which was broken and strengthen that which was sick. Eze. 34:16
  - "I will. Be clean." Mt. 8:3
  - He took my infirmities. Mt. 8:17
  - Me bore my sicknesses. Mt. 8:17

- FRIDAY:
  - He heals the sick. Mt. 14:14
  - He heals all manner of sickness and all manner of disease. Mt. 4:23
  - According to my faith, let it be unto me. Mt. 9:29
  - He gives me power and authority to cast out, to heal all manner of sickness and disease. Mt. 10:1, Lk. 9:1
  - He heals them. Mt. 12:15, Hebr. 13:8
  - As many as touch Him are made perfectly whole. Mt. 14:36
  - Greater things than these you will do. John 14:12-14

- SATURDAY:
  - He heals all those who have need of healing. Lk. 9:11
  - He is come that I might have life abundantly. Jm. 10:10

- If I ask anything in His name, He will do it. Jn. 14:14
- Jesus Christ makes me whole. Acts 9:34
- He does good and heals all that are oppressed of the devil. Acts 10:38
- The law of the Spirit of life in Him has made me free from the law of sin and death. Rom. 8:2

- SUNDAY:
  - If I rightly discern His body, which was broken for me, and judge myself, I'll not be judged, and I'll not be weak, sickly, or die prematurely. 1 Cor. 11:29-31
  - He has delivered me from the authority of darkness. Col. 1:13
  - By His stripes I was healed. 1 Pet. 2:24
  - His divine power has given me all things that pertain to life and godliness through the knowledge of Him. 2 Pet. 1:3
  - These signs shall follow – you will lay hands and bring healing. Mark 16:15-18

APPENDIX D

– Verses on the Spoken Word (These verses are KJV. I would encourage you to personalize them for your own use.)
– (James 3:5) **"Even so the tongue is a little member, and boasteth great things. Behold,**
– **how great a matter a little fire kindleth!"**
– (Ephesians 4:29) **"Let no corrupt communication proceed out of your mouth, but that which is good to the use of edifying, that it may minister grace unto the hearers."**
– (Romans 4:17) **"(As it is written, I have made thee a father of many nations,) before him whom he believed,** *even* **God, who quickeneth the dead, and calleth those things which be not as though they were."**
– (Mark 4:37-40) **"And there arose a great storm of wind, and the waves beat into the ship, so that it was now full. And he was in the hinder part of the ship, asleep on a pillow: and they awake him, and say unto him, Master, carest thou not that we perish? And he arose, and rebuked the wind, and said unto the sea, Peace, be still. And the wind ceased, and there was a great calm. And he said unto them, Why are ye so fearful? how is it that ye have no faith?"**
– (Romans 10:10) **"For with the heart man**

believeth unto righteousness; and with the mouth confession is made unto salvation."

- (John 6:68) "Then Simon Peter answered him, Lord, to whom shall we go? Thou hast the words of eternal life."
- (Matthew 15:18) "...those things which proceed out of the mouth come forth from the heart; and they defile the man."
- (Proverbs 18:21) "Death and life *are* in the power of the tongue: and they that love it shall eat the fruit thereof."
- (Romans 4:17) "For they eat the bread of wickedness, and drink the wine of violence."
- (Proverbs 13:3) "He that keepeth his mouth keepeth his life: *but* he that openeth wide his lips shall have destruction."
- (Proverbs 18:7) "A fool's mouth is his destruction, and his lips *are* the snare of his soul."
- (James 3:6) "And the tongue is a fire, a world of iniquity: so is the tongue among our members, that it defileth the whole body, and setteth on fire the course of nature; and it is set on fire of hell."
- The Lord God honors His word highly, (Psalm 138:2) and is looking out for it to perform it. (Jeremiah, 1:12).
- (Matt. 12:34-36) "O generation of vipers, how can ye, being evil, speak good things? For out of the abundance of the heart the

mouth speaketh. A good man out of the good treasure of the heart bringeth forth good things: and an evil man out of the evil treasure bringeth forth evil things. But I say unto you, That every idle word that men shall speak, they shall give account thereof in the day of judgment."

– (Job 3:25) "For the thing which I greatly feared is come upon me, and that which I was afraid of is come unto me."

– (Proverbs 18:20-21) "A man's belly shall be satisfied with the fruit of his mouth; *and* with the increase of his lips shall he be filled. Death and life *are* in the power of the tongue: and they that love it shall eat the fruit thereof."

– (Proverbs 12:18) "There is that speaketh like the piercings of a sword: but the tongue of the wise *is* health."

– (Mark 11:22-23) "And Jesus answering saith unto them, Have faith in God. For verily I say unto you, That whosoever shall say unto this mountain, Be thou removed, and be thou cast into the sea; and shall not doubt in his heart, but shall believe that those things which he saith shall come to pass; he shall have whatsoever he saith."

– (Matthew 12:36-37) "But I say unto you, That every idle word that men shall speak, they shall give account thereof in the day of judgment. For by thy words thou shalt be justified, and by thy words thou shalt be condemned."

- (Ephesians 4:29) "Let no corrupt communication proceed out of your mouth, but that which is good to the use of edifying, that it may minister grace unto the hearers."
- (Isaiah 57:19) "I create the fruit of the lips..."
- (James 3:8) "But the tongue can no man tame; *it is* an unruly evil, full of deadly poison."
- (Colossians 4:6) "Let your speech *be* always with grace, seasoned with salt, that ye may know how ye ought to answer every man."
- (Matthew 4:4) "But he answered and said, It is written, Man shall not live by bread alone, but by every word that proceedeth out of the mouth of God."
- (Isaiah 57:19) "I create the fruit of the lips; Peace, peace to *him that* is far off, and to *him that is* near, saith the LORD; and I will heal him."
- (Romans 10:17) "So then faith *cometh* by hearing, and hearing by the word of God."
- (Psalm 19:14) "Let the words of my mouth, and the meditation of my heart, be acceptable in thy sight, O LORD, my strength, and my redeemer."
- (Proverbs 12:14) "A man shall be satisfied with good by the fruit of *his* mouth: and the recompense of a man's hands shall be rendered unto him."

APPENDIX E

Verses on Prosperity

(Most of these verses I have placed here in a personalized format to give you an idea of how we can make them our own.)

- (Prov. 3:9) **"Honor the LORD with thy substance, and with the firstfruits of all thine increase:"**
- (Phil. 4:19) **"But my God shall supply all your need according to his riches in glory by Christ Jesus."**
- (Matt. 6:33) **"But seek ye first the kingdom of God, and his righteousness; and all these things shall be added unto you."**
- (Psalm 112:1-3) **"Praise ye the LORD. Blessed** *is* **the man** *that* **feareth the LORD,** *that* **delighteth greatly in his commandments. His seed shall be mighty upon earth: the generation of the upright** *shall be* **blessed. Wealth and riches shall be in his house: and his righteousness endureth for ever."**
- (Jeremiah 29:11-14) **"For I know the thoughts that I think toward you, saith the LORD, thoughts of peace, and not of evil, to give you an expected end. Then shall ye call upon me, and ye shall go and pray unto me, and I will hearken unto you. And ye shall seek**

me, and find *me*, when ye shall search for me with all your heart. And I will be found of you, saith the LORD: and I will turn away your captivity, and I will gather you from all the nations, and from all the places whither I have driven you, saith the LORD; and I will bring you again into the place whence I caused you to be carried away captive."

- (Psalm 144:12-15) "That our sons *may be* as plants grown up in their youth; that our daughters may be as corner stones, polished *after* the similitude of a palace: *That* our garners may be full, affording all manner of store: that our sheep may bring forth thousands and ten thousands in our streets: *That* our oxen *may be* strong to labor; *that there be* no breaking in, nor going out; that *there be* no complaining in our streets. Happy *is that* people, that is in such a case: yea, happy *is that* people, whose God is the LORD."

- (Prov. 13:21-22) "Evil pursueth sinners: but to the righteous good shall be repaid. A good *man* leaveth an inheritance to his children's children: and the wealth of the sinner is laid up for the just."

- (2 Cor. 8:9) "For ye know the grace of our Lord Jesus Christ, that, though he was rich, yet for your sakes he became poor, that ye through his poverty might be rich."

- (Deut. 28:10-13) "And all people of the earth

shall see that thou art called by the name of the LORD; and they shall be afraid of thee. And the LORD shall make thee plenteous in goods, in the fruit of thy body, and in the fruit of thy cattle, and in the fruit of thy ground, in the land which the LORD sware unto thy fathers to give thee. The LORD shall open unto thee his good treasure, the heaven to give the rain unto thy land in his season, and to bless all the work of thine hand: and thou shalt lend unto many nations, and thou shalt not borrow. And the LORD shall make thee the head, and not the tail; and thou shalt be above only, and thou shalt not be beneath; if that thou hearken unto the commandments of the LORD thy God, which I command thee this day, to observe and to do *them*:"

– (Psalm 5:12) "**For thou, LORD, wilt bless the righteous; with favor wilt thou compass him as *with* a shield.**"

– (Psalm 1:3) "**And he shall be like a tree planted by the rivers of water, that bringeth forth his fruit in his season; his leaf also shall not wither; and whatsoever he doeth shall prosper.**"

– (Prov. 3:9) "**Honor the LORD with thy substance, and with the firstfruits of all thine increase:**"

– (Phil. 4:19) "**But my God shall supply all your need according to his riches in glory by**

Christ Jesus."

- (Matt. 6:33) "But seek ye first the kingdom of God, and his righteousness; and all these things shall be added unto you."

- (Psalm 112:1-3) "Praise ye the LORD. Blessed *is* the man *that* feareth the LORD, *that* delighteth greatly in his commandments. His seed shall be mighty upon earth: the generation of the upright shall be blessed. Wealth and riches *shall be* in his house: and his righteousness endureth for ever."

- (Jeremiah 29:11-14) "For I know the thoughts that I think toward you, saith the LORD, thoughts of peace, and not of evil, to give you an expected end. Then shall ye call upon me, and ye shall go and pray unto me, and I will hearken unto you. And ye shall seek me, and find me, when ye shall search for me with all your heart. And I will be found of you, saith the LORD: and I will turn away your captivity, and I will gather you from all the nations, and from all the places whither I have driven you, saith the LORD; and I will bring you again into the place whence I caused you to be carried away captive."

- (Psalm 144:12-15) "That our sons *may be as* plants grown up in their youth; *that* our daughters *may be* as corner stones, polished after the similitude of a palace: *That* our garners may be full, affording all manner

of store: *that* our sheep may bring forth
thousands and ten thousands in our streets:
That our oxen may be strong to labor; that
there be no breaking in, nor going out; that
there be no complaining in our streets.
Happy is that people, that is in such a case:
yea, happy is that people, whose God is the
LORD."

– (Prov. 13:21-22) "Evil pursueth sinners: but
to the righteous good shall be repaid. A good
man leaveth an inheritance to his children's
children: and the wealth of the sinner is laid
up for the just."

– (2 Cor. 8:9) "For ye know the grace of our
Lord Jesus Christ, that, though he was rich,
yet for your sakes he became poor, that ye
through his poverty might be rich"

– (Deut. 28:10-13) "And all people of the earth
shall see that thou art called by the name of
the LORD; and they shall be afraid of thee.
And the LORD shall make thee plenteous in
goods, in the fruit of thy body, and in the fruit
of thy cattle, and in the fruit of thy ground,
in the land which the LORD sware unto thy
fathers to give thee. The LORD shall open
unto thee his good treasure, the heaven to
give the rain unto thy land in his season, and
to bless all the work of thine hand: and thou
shalt lend unto many nations, and thou shalt
not borrow. And the LORD shall make thee

the head, and not the tail; and thou shalt be above only, and thou shalt not be beneath; if that thou hearken unto the commandments of the LORD thy God, which I command thee this day, to observe and to do *them*:"

- - (Psalm 5:12) "**For thou, LORD, wilt bless the righteous; with favor wilt thou compass him as** *with* **a shield.**"

- (Psalm 1:3) "**And he shall be like a tree planted by the rivers of water, that bringeth forth his fruit in his season; his leaf also shall not wither; and whatsoever he doeth shall prosper.**"

- (Proverbs 17:27-28) "**He that hath knowledge spareth his words:** *and* **a man of understanding is of an excellent spirit. Even a fool, when he holdeth his peace, is counted wise:** *and* **he that shutteth his lips** *is esteemed* **a man of understanding.**"